THE HAPPINESS AMPLIFIER

The Neuroscience and Psychology of Happiness. Holistic Happiness Transformation and Elevated Quality of Life. Master the 7 Secrets of Blissful living.

GIRENDRA NATH SINGH

Your Free Gift

As a token of my thanks for taking time to read my book, I would like to offer you a free gift:

Click Here or scan the below QR Code to Receive your Free Book:

https://gnsingh.ck.page/79606d929c

Discover a life transformed by joy! Dive into **"The Happiness Amplifier"** a groundbreaking exploration that merges psychology, neuroscience, and real-life insights to guide you on a journey towards a profoundly fulfilled existence.

✸ Are you ready to embark on a path that leads to sustained happiness and fulfillment? Look no further!

In a world where happiness is often elusive, this meticulously crafted masterpiece will be your ultimate guide. Uncover the secrets that have the potential to revolutionize your life, leaving you brimming with lasting joy and contentment.

What Awaits You?

- ❖ **Journey into the Heart of Happiness:** Delve into the depths of why happiness is more than just a fleeting emotion. Explore its multifaceted dimensions and how it influences your overall well-being, relationships, and personal growth.

- ❖ **Unveiling the Neurochemical Symphony:** Immerse yourself in the fascinating world of brain chemistry. **Understand the roles of serotonin, dopamine, oxytocin, and endorphins** in shaping your emotions and experiences. Discover how to harness these **neurochemical powerhouses** to amplify your happiness naturally.

- ❖ **Mastering the Art of Positive Habits:** Unearth the transformative potential of habits. Learn how they reshape your brain, influence your emotions, and ultimately sculpt your life. ***Dive into practical strategies to identify and overcome negative patterns***, creating a pathway to sustained joy.

- ❖ **The External Tapestry of Joy:** Explore the impact of your environment on your happiness. From nurturing social connections to curating a harmonious space, unveil how external factors shape your well-being. Find your purpose by aligning your passions with meaningful pursuits.

- ❖ **Amplifying Serotonin:** Discover evidence-based techniques to naturally increase serotonin levels. Dive into lifestyle choices, dietary habits, and cognitive practices that cultivate sustained well-being. Elevate your mood and experience a heightened sense of joy.

- ❖ **Pursuit of Passion and Purpose:** Uncover the magic of pursuing what sets your soul on fire. Tap into the realm of passion and purpose, where fulfillment transcends momentary pleasures. Experience a life rich with meaning and profound satisfaction.

- ❖ **Your Journey to Sustainable Joy:** As you weave through each chapter, a transformative journey unfolds. Gain insights into the interplay between **brain chemistry, habits, and external influences,** guiding you towards a life marked by **resilience, positivity, and radiant joy.**

Why Choose "The Happiness Amplifier"?

➢ **Scientific Rigor Meets Real-Life Stories:** Immerse yourself in a harmonious blend of rigorous scientific research and heartwarming real-life narratives. Witness the transformative power of happiness through relatable experiences.

➢ **Actionable Strategies:** This is not just a book; it's your guide to action. Each chapter equips you with practical techniques to amplify your well-being. Embrace the power of change and witness the profound shifts in your life.

➢ **Embrace a Life of Fulfillment:** Say goodbye to the fleeting pursuit of happiness. Embrace a life where joy is not just an emotion but a sustainable state of being. This book holds the keys to unlocking the doors to a life of profound contentment and lasting happiness.

Are you ready to rewrite your story and embark on a journey of transformation?

Your adventure towards a life filled with radiant happiness starts here!

CONTENTS

Chapter 1: Introduction

"The purpose of our lives is to be happy." - Dalai Lama

****

Shifting Shades of Life: Discovering Joy amidst Sorrows

There lived a man who was very unhappy with his life. He was always full of sorrows, and because of this, he was always sad. One day, one of his friends told him that a wise monk was staying in a nearby town for a few days, and he suggested that the man meet the monk for his problems. Initially, the man was reluctant to meet the monk, but then he thought that there was no harm in meeting the monk. So, he decided to meet the monk.

The next day, the man went to see the monk at his place. When the man entered the room, he saw that the monk had just finished his meditation and was sitting peacefully on a simple cloth mat. The man bowed down to him and sat in front of him. Then he said, "Sir, my life is full of sorrows." He then proceeded to list the problems he had to the monk one by one. Continuing, the man said, "Sir, I have so many problems in my life due to which I am always sad. Please give me some solutions." After that, the man became silent and started waiting for the monk to speak.

The monk looked at the man with compassion, thought for a moment, and then he said, "My friend, can you tell me how many red colors are in this room?" The man was surprised to hear this from the monk. He was thinking, "I am asking for a solution for my problem, and this monk is asking me unnecessary questions." But still, unwillingly, he looked around the room, counted red colors in the room, and then said, "Sir, there are many things in this room which are that color." He then explained, "Sir, this pillow is red, that apple is red, that mat is red, and your slippers are also red. Apart from that, there are many red-colored things in this room."

The monk said, "Okay, now without looking anywhere, tell me how many blue colors are in this room." The man was confused, listening to this. He then said, "Sir, how can I tell you without seeing again?" The Zen master asked, "When you were looking for red color, did you not notice blue color then?" The man said, "No, sir. When I was looking for red color, I was focused only on that color. Therefore, I could not notice the blue color in this room."

Listening to this, the monk smiled and said, "My friend, this is the answer to your question. Our life is also like that. You will get what you look for. While you are looking for red color in this room, your mind was totally focused on finding that color. You could not see any other color. There are many things in this room which are blue. But you were so focused on the red color that you could not notice it. Similarly, our life is also a combination of both happiness and sorrow. But you have focused your attention so much on the sorrows in your life that you don't see happiness in your life.

Happiness and sorrows are two sides of a coin. If there is no happiness in life, then how can there be a feeling of sorrow? Similarly, if there is no sorrow in life, then how can there be a feeling of happiness? Therefore, change your perspective of looking at life.

Try to find moments of happiness in your life. If you focus your attention on happiness instead of sorrows, then you will find that life is full of happiness. Life is a combination of both happiness and sorrow. What matters is what we focus our attention on. If you look for happiness in your life, you will get happiness, and if you look for sorrows, you will get sorrow. Therefore, always try to find happiness even in the smallest things in your life. Remember that every moment that is passing by will never come back. *So why not live this moment happily rather than being sad?*

≈ ≈ ≈

In a world filled with ever-increasing demands, complexities, and uncertainties, the pursuit of happiness has become a universal aspiration. People of all ages, cultures, and backgrounds seek happiness as an essential ingredient for a fulfilling and meaningful life. Yet, the very nature of happiness often eludes us, leaving us in a perpetual search for something we cannot quite grasp. **"The Happiness Amplifier"** sets out to unravel this enigmatic emotion, shedding light on the factors that truly amplify happiness and offering evidence-based strategies to cultivate sustainable joy.

A. Importance of Happiness and Well-being: Happiness is not merely a fleeting emotion but a state of being that influences our thoughts, actions, and overall health. Research in psychology and neuroscience has repeatedly shown the far-reaching impact of happiness on physical health, mental well-being, cognitive abilities, and social relationships. Thus, it is crucial to explore the science of happiness to understand its complexities fully.

The importance of happiness and well-being in human life cannot be overstated. Beyond the pursuit of material success and achievements, happiness stands as a fundamental aspect of human existence, shaping our overall quality of life and influencing our physical, mental, and social well-being.

B. The Science of Happiness: Psychology and Neuroscience.

The science of happiness is a multidisciplinary field that draws on insights from both psychology and neuroscience to understand the complexities of this elusive emotion. By exploring the interplay between these two disciplines, researchers have made significant strides in unraveling the mechanisms underlying happiness and its impact on human cognition, behavior, and well-being.

Integrating Psychology and Neuroscience:

The integration of psychology and neuroscience in the study of happiness allows researchers to bridge the gap between subjective experiences and underlying neural mechanisms. This multidisciplinary approach provides a more comprehensive understanding of how happiness is generated, regulated, and influenced by various factors.

The collaboration between psychology and neuroscience has paved the way for evidence-based interventions to enhance happiness and well-being. Techniques like **cognitive-behavioral therapy (CBT)**, mindfulness-based interventions, and positive psychology interventions are rooted in scientific research and have shown promising results in promoting sustained happiness.

QUIZ TIME

1. Why is it important to prioritize happiness and well-being in our lives?

A) To impress others with our positive attitude.

B) To achieve financial success and material possessions.

C) To lead a more fulfilling and meaningful life.

D) To gain recognition and fame.

2. How does happiness impact our physical health?

A) It weakens the immune system.

B) It has no effect on physical health.

C) It improves overall well-being and strengthens the immune system.

D) It leads to higher stress levels.

3. What about the relationship between happiness and resilience?

A) Happiness has no influence on resilience.

B) Happiness makes people more susceptible to setbacks.

C) Happiness contributes to greater resilience and the ability to bounce back from challenges.

D) Resilience has no connection with happiness.

4. **What are some evidence-based strategies to increase happiness in our lives?**

A) Avoiding all forms of stress.

 B) Surrounding ourselves with material possessions.

C) Practicing gratitude and nurturing meaningful relationships.

D) Focusing solely on personal achievements.

5. **How does happiness impact our decision-making abilities?**

A) It impairs decision-making.

B) It has no effect on decision-making.

C) It enhances cognitive functions, leading to better decision-making.

D) Happiness leads to impulsive decisions.

Answers: All (C)

****

Chapter 2: Understanding Happiness

"Happiness is not in the mere possession of money; it lies in the joy of achievement, in the thrill of creative effort." - Franklin D. Roosevelt

****

The Alchemy of Attitude: Turning Labor into Pure Happiness

Once upon a time, a monk was passing by a village. Just then, he saw that some men were working with stones. The monk went to a man working there and asked, "What is being made here?" The man replied angrily, "Don't you see that I am cutting stones?" Again, the monk asked, "Yes, I can see, but I am asking what is being made here?" The man shouted, "I don't know. I am dying here, working in the heat, and you are worried about what will be made here. Just leave from here."

Listening to this, the monk moved forward. He went to another man working there and asked, "What is being made here?" The man replied, "I am working for money. I will get some money as a daily wage, and that's what matters to me. I have no idea what is being made here."

The monk moved forward and saw another man working there. He went to him and asked, "What is being made here?" The man smiled and replied, "We are making a temple here." The monk asked, "You look so happy. Don't you feel tired working here on such a hot day?" The man replied, "No, I don't feel tired." Then he continued, "There is no big temple in this village, and because of that, the people of this village have to go to another village to pray and celebrate. I also belong to this village. When I hit a stone with a chisel, I hear melodious music in the sound of that hit. I feel blessed. I imagine that after a few days, when the temple construction will be completed and ready to be worshipped, prayers will be held here, and the people of this village will be able to come here for singing prayers."

"When I think about how much happiness it will bring to the people who will come in here, all this work does not feel like work to me. I feel like I am having fun. I find this work as a service to the Almighty. When I go home in the evening, I feel satisfied. I sleep at night with the imagination of the temple and wake up in the morning with enthusiasm, ready to cut pillars for the temple. Sometimes I start singing devotional songs while working. I have never enjoyed working so much in my life."

After listening to the man, the monk smiled, tapped the man on his shoulder, and left from there. On the way, he was thinking, ***"This is the secret of a happy life. It is just a difference of thinking and opinion. Someone is considering the work as a burden and spending their whole life complaining, while someone else is enjoying life by considering the same work as fun and pleasure."***

"In our lives, we will find that this is the way to live a happy life. When we do our every work with trust and enthusiasm, our whole life can be filled with happiness. Most of the people in the world do their work unwillingly and without interest, and for this reason, neither their work is done properly nor do they find pleasure in doing so. Such people can never become successful in their lives. On the other hand, those who do their work with great interest and enthusiasm not only do their work perfectly, but they also find pleasure in doing so. We should remember that work is our worship."

≈ ≈ ≈

Understanding happiness is a multifaceted endeavor that involves exploring the nature of happiness, its impact on human life, and the factors that contribute to its experience. Elaborating on the concept of understanding happiness reveals key insights into this complex and vital emotion:

A. The Nature of Happiness: What is it and how does it affect our lives?

The nature of happiness is a complex and multifaceted concept that encompasses positive emotional experiences, life satisfaction, and overall well-being. It is a fundamental human emotion that influences various aspects of our lives, impacting our physical health, mental well-being, cognitive functioning, social interactions, and overall quality of life. Exploring the nature of happiness in detail provides a deeper understanding of its significance and its effects on human life:

1. Components of Happiness:

A. Positive Emotions: At its core, happiness involves experiencing positive emotions, such as joy, gratitude, love, excitement, and contentment. These emotions contribute to feelings of pleasure, satisfaction, and overall well-being. Positive emotions act as signals of happiness, indicating that individuals are experiencing moments of delight and fulfillment.

B. Life Satisfaction: Happiness is not solely dependent on momentary feelings of pleasure; it also encompasses a cognitive evaluation of one's life satisfaction. It involves overall contentment and a sense of fulfillment with one's life as a whole. Life satisfaction reflects an individual's assessment of their achievements, relationships, and personal goals.

2. Effects on Physical Health:

A. Immune System: Happiness has been linked to a strengthened immune system. Positive emotions can enhance the function of immune cells, leading to better defense against infections and illnesses.

B. Cardiovascular Health: Studies have shown that happiness and well-being are associated with improved cardiovascular health. Happier individuals tend to have lower blood pressure, reduced risk of heart disease, and a decreased likelihood of experiencing adverse cardiac events.

C. Pain Management: Positive emotions can act as natural pain relievers. Happiness triggers the release of endorphins, the body's natural painkillers, which can help reduce discomfort and enhance pain tolerance.

3. Impact on Mental Well-being:

A. Resilience: Happiness contributes to greater psychological resilience, helping individuals cope with stress, challenges, and setbacks more effectively. Happy individuals tend to bounce back from adversity and maintain a positive outlook on life.

B. Mental Health: Happiness is linked to better mental health outcomes, including reduced risk of depression, anxiety, and other psychological disorders. Positive emotions serve as protective factors against mental health issues.

C. Cognitive Functioning: Studies have shown that happiness enhances cognitive abilities, including memory, attention, and problem-solving. Positive emotions can improve cognitive flexibility and creativity, leading to better decision-making skills.

4. Influence on Social Interactions:

A. Social Connections: Happiness is closely intertwined with social relationships. Happier individuals are more likely to attract and maintain meaningful friendships and romantic partnerships. Positive emotions also contribute to more satisfying and harmonious interactions with others.

B. Prosocial Behavior: Happy individuals tend to engage in more prosocial behaviors, such as acts of kindness and altruism. Positive emotions foster empathy and compassion, leading to a greater willingness to help others.

5. Overall Quality of Life:

A. Subjective Well-being: Happiness is a key component of subjective well-being, which refers to an individual's overall evaluation of their own life and happiness. High levels of subjective well-being are associated with a greater sense of fulfillment and life satisfaction.

B. Meaning and Purpose: Happiness is intertwined with a sense of meaning and purpose in life. Eudemonic happiness, which focuses on pursuing meaningful goals and contributing to something larger than oneself, adds depth and fulfillment to one's happiness.

B. The Role of Brain Chemistry: Serotonin, Dopamine, Oxytocin, and Endorphins.

The role of brain chemistry is essential in understanding the underlying biological mechanisms that contribute to happiness and well-being. Several key neurotransmitters play a significant role in regulating our emotions, mood, and pleasure sensations. These neurotransmitters include **serotonin, dopamine, oxytocin, and endorphins.** Each of these chemicals has specific functions in the brain that influence our emotional experiences and overall state of happiness. Let's explore the role of each neurotransmitter in detail:

Serotonin: Serotonin is often referred to as the **"happy chemical"** because of its role in regulating mood and promoting feelings of well-being and happiness. It is a **neurotransmitter** that is primarily produced in the brain and the digestive system. Serotonin influences various physiological and psychological processes, including:

- **Mood Regulation:** Serotonin helps to stabilize mood and prevent mood fluctuations. Adequate levels of serotonin are associated with a more stable and positive emotional state.

- **Anxiety and Depression:** Low levels of serotonin have been linked to conditions such as anxiety and depression. Antidepressant medications, known as

selective serotonin reuptake inhibitors (SSRIs), work by increasing serotonin levels in the brain.

- **Sleep and Appetite:** Serotonin plays a role in regulating sleep patterns and appetite. It is involved in the sleep-wake cycle and can influence feelings of satisfaction after eating.

Strategies to Increase Serotonin Naturally:

- Engaging in regular exercise, particularly aerobic activities, has been shown to boost serotonin levels.

- Spending time outdoors and getting exposure to natural sunlight can also increase serotonin production.

- Practicing mindfulness and meditation has been associated with higher serotonin levels and improved mood.

Dopamine: Dopamine is often referred to as the **"reward chemical"** because of its role in the brain's reward and pleasure system. It is released in response to pleasurable experiences and reinforces behaviors that lead to rewards. Dopamine is involved in several functions, including:

- **Reward and Pleasure:** Dopamine is released when we experience pleasurable activities such as eating delicious food, engaging in enjoyable hobbies, or receiving social recognition.

- **Motivation and Goal Pursuit:** Dopamine plays a crucial role in motivation and goal-directed behavior. It drives us to pursue rewards and achieve our objectives.
- **Learning and Memory:** Dopamine is involved in the process of reinforcement learning, helping us remember rewarding experiences and motivating us to repeat them.

Strategies to Increase Dopamine Naturally:

- Setting and achieving meaningful goals can increase dopamine levels and provide a sense of accomplishment and reward.
- Engaging in creative activities and hobbies that bring joy and satisfaction can boost dopamine release.
- Practicing gratitude and expressing appreciation for positive experiences can also elevate dopamine levels.

Oxytocin: Oxytocin is often referred to as the **"love hormone" or "bonding hormone"** because of its role in social bonding, trust, and affectionate relationships. Oxytocin is released in response to social interactions and acts on various brain regions, including:

- **Social Bonding:** Oxytocin is released during positive social interactions, such as hugging, cuddling, and spending time with loved ones. It fosters feelings of trust and attachment.

- **Parent-Child Bonding:** Oxytocin plays a critical role in promoting bonding between parents and their children, contributing to parental care and nurturing behavior.

Strategies to Increase Oxytocin Naturally:

- Engaging in social activities and spending quality time with loved ones can trigger the release of oxytocin.
- Acts of kindness and altruistic behavior, such as helping others, can also increase oxytocin levels.

- Physical touch, such as hugging or holding hands, has been shown to stimulate oxytocin release.

Endorphins: Endorphins are often referred to as **"natural painkillers"** because of their ability to reduce pain and promote feelings of euphoria. Endorphins are released in response to stress and pain, acting as the body's natural pain management system. Their role includes:

- **Pain Relief:** Endorphins bind to opioid receptors in the brain and spinal cord, blocking pain signals and reducing discomfort.

- **Euphoria and Pleasure:** Endorphins are associated with feelings of euphoria and pleasure, contributing to the **"runner's high"** experienced during intense exercise.

- **Stress Reduction:** Endorphins are released during stress and can help alleviate feelings of anxiety and tension.

Strategies to Increase Endorphins Naturally:

- Engaging in physical activities, particularly aerobic exercises, can trigger the release of endorphins and improve mood.

- Laughter is known to stimulate the release of endorphins and promote feelings of happiness and well-being.

- Engaging in enjoyable activities, such as listening to music or spending time with pets, can also increase endorphin levels.

The role of brain chemistry, involving neurotransmitters such as **serotonin, dopamine, oxytocin, and endorphins,** plays a crucial role in regulating emotions, mood, and pleasure sensations. These **neurotransmitters** influence various aspects of our lives, including mood regulation, motivation, social bonding, pain management, and stress reduction. Understanding the functions of these neurotransmitters allows us to explore evidence-based strategies to naturally boost their levels and enhance our overall state of happiness and well-being.

C. The Hedonic Treadmill: Why lasting happiness is challenging.

The hedonic treadmill, also known as hedonic adaptation, refers to the phenomenon where individuals' levels of happiness and life satisfaction tend to return to a relatively stable baseline over time, despite experiencing positive or negative life events.

The concept is derived from the idea that people continuously seek to improve their well-being and pursue things they believe will make them happier. However, as they attain these goals or experience positive changes, they quickly adapt to the new circumstances, and the initial boost in happiness becomes temporary. This adaptation process prevents individuals from experiencing a lasting increase in happiness and contributes to the ongoing pursuit of external sources of happiness. Several factors contribute to why lasting happiness is challenging due to the hedonic treadmill:

1. Habituation and Novelty: When individuals experience positive events or acquire new possessions, they initially feel a surge of happiness and pleasure. However, over time, they become accustomed to these positive changes, and the positive emotions diminish. This habituation to positive stimuli reduces the impact of the event or possession on long-term happiness.

2. Relative Comparison: People often evaluate their happiness relative to others or their previous states. As a result, even if they experience positive changes, they may still feel unsatisfied if they perceive that others are happier or if they have experienced greater happiness in the past. This relative comparison can prevent you from achieving a stable, lasting increase in happiness.

3. Changing Aspirations and Goals: As you achieve your goals or acquire possessions you once desired, your aspirations and goals tend to change. You set new benchmarks for happiness and well-being, leading to an ongoing pursuit of the next desire. This constant striving for more prevents you from reaching a state of lasting contentment.

4. Adaptation to Positive and Negative Events: The hedonic treadmill applies not only to positive events but also to negative ones. While you may experience a temporary decrease in happiness due to negative events, you often adapt and return to your baseline level of happiness over time. This ability to adapt to negative circumstances can be beneficial for coping with adversity but may hinder lasting increases in happiness.

5. Diminishing Marginal Utility: The concept of diminishing marginal utility suggests that the more you consume or experience something, the less additional happiness or satisfaction you gain from each additional unit. For example, the first piece of chocolate may bring immense pleasure, but subsequent pieces may provide diminishing increments of happiness. This phenomenon makes it challenging to sustain long-term increases in happiness through material consumption.

Despite the challenges posed by the hedonic treadmill, you can still find ways to experience lasting happiness and well-being:

- **Cultivating Gratitude:** Practicing gratitude and appreciating what you already have can counteract the adaptation to positive events and enhance overall well-being.

- **Fostering Social Connections:** Investing in meaningful relationships and social connections can provide a stable source of happiness and support.

- **Pursuing Meaning and Purpose:** Engaging in activities that align with your values and contribute to a sense of purpose can lead to deeper and more lasting satisfaction.

- **Mindfulness and Enjoyment of the Present:** Being mindful of the present moment and savoring positive experiences can help you fully appreciate and derive lasting happiness from them.

The **hedonic treadmill** poses a challenge to achieving lasting happiness as you tend to adapt to positive changes and revert to a stable baseline level of happiness over time. The pursuit of external sources of happiness, habituation to positive events, and changing aspirations contribute to this adaptation process. Despite these challenges, understanding the nature of the hedonic treadmill empowers you to seek more sustainable sources of happiness, such as gratitude, social connections, and a sense of meaning and purpose, to experience lasting well-being and contentment in your life.

QUIZ TIME

1. What is the main focus of, "The Science of Happiness: Psychology and Neuroscience"?

A) Understanding the impact of external factors on happiness.

B) Examining the role of brain chemistry in happiness.

C) Exploring the influence of social connections on happiness.

D) Analyzing the relationship between happiness and physical health.

2. Which neurotransmitters are discussed as key players in happiness?

A) Serotonin, Dopamine, and Endorphins.

 B) Oxytocin, Dopamine, and Adrenaline.

C) Endorphins, Cortisol, and Serotonin.

D) Dopamine, Serotonin, and Adrenaline.

3. What is the role of serotonin in happiness?

A) Serotonin contributes to the fight-or-flight response in stressful situations.

B) Serotonin is responsible for feelings of pleasure and reward.

 C) Serotonin regulates mood and plays a crucial role in promoting happiness.

D) Serotonin has no impact on emotional well-being.

4. What is the function of dopamine?

A) Dopamine helps in regulating sleep patterns.

 B) Dopamine is responsible for feelings of happiness and pleasure.

 C) Dopamine has no role in emotional experiences.

D) Dopamine controls the body's response to stress.

5. How do endorphins contribute to our sense of happiness?

A) Endorphins regulate the body's immune response.

B) Endorphins have no impact on emotional well-being.

 C) Endorphins reduce pain and induce feelings of euphoria and happiness.

D) Endorphins cause feelings of stress and anxiety.

Answer: 1. (B), 2 (A) 3 (C) 4 (B) 5 (C)

****

Chapter 3: The Interplay of Brain Chemistry and Habits

"The key to happiness is the acceptance of the present moment." - Eckhart Tolle

****

The Monk's Coin: A Tale of Perspective and Contentment

Once a monk was passing through the capital city of a famous king. While he was walking, he saw a single currency coin lying on the road. He picked it up. Satisfied with his simple living and having no use for the coin, he thought of donating it to someone in need.

He strolled around the streets throughout the day, asking people to take the coin, but he did not find anyone who needed it. Finally, he reached a rest area and spent the night there. The next morning, he woke up for his daily activities and noticed that the king was preparing to invade another state with his army.

When the king saw the monk standing, he ordered his army to halt. He approached the monk and said, "Oh wise one, I am going to war to conquer another state and expand my territory, increasing my wealth. Please bless me to be victorious."

After a moment of contemplation, the monk took out the coin and gave it to the king. The king was confused and annoyed, wondering why he was being given a single coin when he was already one of the richest kings. Curiously, he asked the monk, "Why are you giving me this coin? What is the meaning of this single coin?"

The monk replied, "Oh great king, I found this coin yesterday while strolling around the streets of your capital. However, I had no use for it as I am content with my life. I decided to donate it to someone in need. I wandered around your capital until evening, but I found no one who required this coin. No one was willing to take it. It seemed that they were content with their lives and possessions. Hence, I found no one to give this coin to. But today, the king of the state still desires to accumulate more and more, unsatisfied with what he already possesses. I felt that you are in need of this coin, so I have given it to you."

Hearing this from the monk, the king felt ashamed and realized his mistake. He abandoned the idea of war. Reflecting on our lives, we can find that this story is relevant to us too. We should all learn to find happiness with what we have. While we might desire more or better things, we shouldn't overlook the chance to appreciate what we already possess. Many people may lack what we have, and others might have more. It's important not to constantly compare our lives with others'. Instead, ***we should be content with our possessions and lead a happy, peaceful life.***

≈ ≈ ≈

The interplay of brain chemistry and habits is a dynamic and influential relationship that significantly impacts our emotions, behavior, and overall well-being. Our brain chemistry, governed by neurotransmitters such as serotonin, dopamine, oxytocin, and endorphins, plays a pivotal role in regulating our emotions and mood.

Simultaneously, our habits, which are ingrained behavioral patterns, have a profound effect on how our brain functions and how neurotransmitters are released.

By understanding this interplay, we can harness the power of positive habits to promote well-being and break negative cycles that hinder our happiness. Cultivating positive habits and being mindful of their impact empowers us to create a positive feedback loop of sustainable well-being and happiness.

Let's explore in detail the interplay between brain chemistry and habits:

A. Neuroplasticity: How the brain changes and adapts.

Neuroplasticity, also known as brain plasticity or neural plasticity, refers to the brain's remarkable ability to change, adapt, and reorganize itself in response to learning, experiences, and environmental influences. It is a fundamental property of the brain that allows it to continually remodel its neural connections and structure throughout a person's life. Neuroplasticity plays a crucial role in various aspects of brain function, cognition, and recovery from injuries. Let's explore the concept of neuroplasticity in detail:

1. Mechanisms of Neuroplasticity:

- **Synaptic Plasticity:** Synapses are the connections between neurons, and synaptic plasticity refers to changes in the strength and efficacy of these connections. Learning and experiences can strengthen or weaken synaptic connections, enabling neural networks to become more efficient in transmitting information.

- **Structural Plasticity:** Structural plasticity involves changes in the physical structure of neurons and their connections. It includes processes like **dendritic branching (formation of new connections), axonal sprouting (growth of new axon branches), and neurogenesis (birth of new neurons).**

Types of Neuroplasticity:

- **Experience-Dependent Plasticity:** This type of plasticity occurs in response to specific experiences and learning. For example, when you learn a new skill, such as playing a musical instrument or acquiring a new language, the corresponding brain areas undergo structural and functional changes to accommodate the new information.

- **Developmental Plasticity:** During early brain development, the brain is highly plastic, allowing it to adapt to the environment and form appropriate connections. This process is critical for learning and acquiring essential skills during childhood.

- **Adaptive Plasticity:** Adaptive plasticity occurs in response to damage or injury to the brain. When certain brain areas are damaged, neighboring regions may take on new functions to compensate for the lost functions, facilitating recovery and rehabilitation.

Learning and Memory:

- **Neuroplasticity** underlies learning and memory processes. As you learn and encode new information, synaptic connections are strengthened in relevant brain areas, creating lasting changes that form the basis of memory.

- **Repetition and Practice:** Repetition and practice are crucial for consolidating learning and memory. Repeatedly engaging in a particular activity or skill strengthens the **neural pathways** associated with that activity.

Environmental Influences:

- Environmental enrichment, which involves exposing the brain to a stimulating and varied environment, has been shown to enhance neuroplasticity. Enriched environments with opportunities for learning, physical activity, and social interaction promote the growth of new neurons and synapses.

- Conversely, a lack of stimulation and limited experiences can lead to a decline in neuroplasticity, affecting cognitive function and brain health.

Neuroplasticity and Brain Rehabilitation:

- Neuroplasticity plays a critical role in brain rehabilitation following injuries or neurological disorders. Through targeted therapies and interventions, the brain can rewire itself to compensate for damaged areas and regain lost functions.

- Techniques such as cognitive training, physical therapy, and occupational therapy leverage neuroplasticity to help patients recover from brain injuries and improve their functional abilities.

Lifelong Plasticity:

- **Contrary to the long-held belief that the brain's plasticity is limited to early childhood, research has demonstrated that neuroplasticity continues throughout life.** While the degree of plasticity may diminish with age, the brain remains capable of adaptation and learning well into old age.

Neuroplasticity is a fundamental property of the brain that allows it to change and adapt in response to experiences, learning, and environmental influences. It involves both synaptic and structural changes in neural connections, enabling the brain to reorganize itself in functional and adaptive ways. Neuroplasticity underlies learning, memory, and brain rehabilitation, making it a crucial factor in shaping cognitive abilities and recovery from injuries. Understanding neuroplasticity has significant implications for education, rehabilitation, and interventions to promote brain health and well-being throughout life.

B. Habits and their Impact on Happiness: The power of routine.

Habits are powerful behavioral patterns that significantly impact our daily lives and overall well-being, including our happiness. These automatic routines and actions can shape our emotions, thoughts, and experiences, making them a crucial factor in determining our level of happiness. Let's explore in detail ***the power of habits*** and their impact on happiness:

1. Habit Formation and the Brain:

- Habits are formed through a process called **"habit formation"**. When we repeatedly engage in a particular behavior in a consistent context, the brain forms neural pathways that make that behavior more automatic and efficient. This process involves the strengthening of synaptic connections in the brain, known as ***synaptic plasticity.***

- Over time, habits become ingrained in our daily routines, and we perform them with little conscious effort or decision-making. This automatic nature of habits allows our brains to conserve cognitive resources and energy.

2. The Role of Habits in Happiness:

- Habits can have a significant impact on our happiness and well-being. Positive habits that promote health, mindfulness, and social connections can contribute to higher levels of happiness.

- For example, engaging in habits such as regular exercise, practicing gratitude, spending time with loved ones, and engaging in hobbies we enjoy can trigger the release of **"happy" neurotransmitters, such as dopamine and endorphins**, promoting positive emotions and well-being.

- On the other hand, negative habits, such as excessive screen time, overconsumption of unhealthy foods, and engaging in constant negative self-talk, can contribute to stress, anxiety, and overall dissatisfaction.

3. Habit Loop and Rewards:

The habit loop consists of three components: **cue, routine, and reward.** Cues are triggers that prompt a habit, routines are the actions themselves, and rewards are the positive reinforcement that follows the behavior.

- To build positive habits that enhance happiness, it's essential to identify the cues that trigger the desired behavior and to create a satisfying reward that reinforces the habit. The brain associates the reward with the routine, making it more likely to be repeated in the future.

4. Breaking Negative Habits:

- Breaking negative habits can be challenging but is crucial for improving happiness and well-being. It involves disrupting the habit loop by identifying and changing the cues that prompt the negative behavior and finding healthier and more fulfilling rewards.

- Replacing negative habits with positive ones that promote well-being and happiness can lead to a positive spiral of improved emotional states and overall life satisfaction.

5. Habit Stacking and Consistency:

- Habit stacking involves linking a new desired habit with an existing one. By attaching a new habit to an already established routine, you are more likely to remember to perform the new behavior consistently.

- Consistency is key to reinforcing habits and creating lasting changes in behavior. Repeating the desired behavior regularly strengthens the associated neural pathways, making the habit more automatic and ingrained.

6. Mindful Habits and Well-being:

- Mindfulness can enhance the power of habits in promoting happiness. Being present and mindful of our actions allows us to choose habits that align with our values and contribute to our well-being.

- Engaging in habits mindfully, rather than on autopilot, allows us to savor positive experiences, fully engage in activities, and make intentional choices that lead to greater happiness.

Habits have a profound impact on our happiness and overall well-being. Positive habits that promote health, social connections, and mindfulness can trigger the release of **"happy" neurotransmitters**, leading to positive emotions and sustained well-being. Breaking negative habits and cultivating positive ones can create a positive feedback loop of happiness and life satisfaction. By understanding the habit loop, incorporating mindful habits, and consistently reinforcing positive behaviors, individuals can harness the power of routine to enhance their happiness and lead fulfilling lives.

C. Identifying and Overcoming Negative Habits.

Identifying and overcoming negative habits is a crucial step in fostering personal growth, improving well-being, and increasing overall happiness. Negative habits can have adverse effects on various aspects of our lives, including our physical health, mental well-being, relationships, and productivity. By recognizing and addressing these habits, we can create positive changes and cultivate a more fulfilling and satisfying life. Here's a detailed guide on how to identify and overcome negative habits:

1. Self-Reflection and Awareness:

- Start by engaging in self-reflection and self-awareness. Take time to observe your daily behaviors and routines without judgment. Pay attention to actions that you feel may be detrimental to your well-being or are not aligned with your long-term goals and values.

- Be honest with yourself and identify patterns of behavior that you would like to change. It could be habits like procrastination, excessive screen time, unhealthy eating, negative self-talk, or any other behavior that negatively impacts your life.

2. Identify Triggers and Cues:

- Triggers and cues are events, emotions, or situations that prompt the negative habit. Recognizing these triggers is crucial in understanding why you engage in the negative habit and how to address it effectively.

- **Keep a journal** or **use a habit-tracking app** to record when the negative habit occurs, what happened before it, and how you felt at the time. Look for patterns and common triggers that may be associated with the habit.

3. Set Clear Goals:

- Establish clear and specific goals for overcoming the negative habit. Define what you want to change, why it is essential to you, and the benefits you expect to gain from breaking the habit.

- Make your goals realistic and achievable. Setting small, incremental milestones can help you build momentum and experience a sense of accomplishment along the way.

4. Implement Replacement Habits:

- Replace the negative habit with a positive alternative that aligns with your goals and values. The new habit should serve as a healthier and more beneficial response to the triggers you identified.

- For example, if stress triggers the negative habit of emotional eating, consider replacing it with relaxation techniques like deep breathing, going for a walk, or practicing mindfulness.

5. Practice Mindfulness:

- Mindfulness plays a crucial role in overcoming negative habits. Be present and aware of your thoughts, emotions, and actions as they arise. When you catch yourself engaging in the negative habit, pause and take a moment to assess whether it aligns with your goals and values.

- Mindfulness can help you gain control over impulsive behaviors and make intentional choices that support your well-being.

6. Build a Support System:

- Share your goals with supportive friends, family members, or a mentor who can encourage and motivate you on your journey to overcome negative habits.

- Having someone to hold you accountable can be beneficial in staying committed to your goals and maintaining progress.

7. Be Patient and Kind to Yourself:

- Breaking negative habits is a process that takes time and effort. Be patient with yourself and understand that setbacks are a normal part of change.

- Avoid self-criticism and practice self-compassion. Treat yourself with kindness and understanding, even when you encounter challenges.

8. Celebrate Progress:

- Acknowledge and celebrate your achievements along the way. Celebrating even small victories can boost your motivation and confidence in overcoming negative habits. Life is a celebration!

Identifying and overcoming negative habits is an empowering process that leads to personal growth and increased happiness. By cultivating self-awareness, recognizing triggers, setting clear goals, implementing replacement habits, and practicing mindfulness, you can break free from negative patterns and build positive behaviors that will contribute to your overall well-being.

Building a support system, being patient with oneself, and celebrating progress are essential aspects of the journey to overcome negative habits successfully.

Remember that change is possible, and with dedication and perseverance, you can create a more fulfilling and satisfying life by letting go of negative habits.

QUIZ TIME

1. How can understanding the interplay of brain chemistry and habits benefit individuals?

A) It has no practical benefits for individuals.

B) It can help individuals develop a daily routine without significance to happiness.

C) It empowers individuals to optimize their habits to enhance happiness and well-being.

D) Understanding brain chemistry and habits is only relevant to neuroscience professionals.

2. How do you define neuroplasticity?

A) Neuroplasticity refers to the ability of the brain to change and adapt over time.

B) Neuroplasticity is a term for brain chemistry changes caused by external factors.

C) Neuroplasticity has no connection with happiness.

D) Neuroplasticity refers to the fixed and unchangeable nature of the brain.

3. How does neuroplasticity contribute to habit formation?

A) Neuroplasticity has no impact on habit formation.

B) Neuroplasticity is solely related to brain injuries.

C) Neuroplasticity allows the brain to rewire itself, strengthening habits through repetition.

D) Neuroplasticity only occurs in individuals with a specific genetic predisposition.

4. What is the connection between habits and happiness?

A) Habits are unrelated to happiness.

B) Habits influence happiness through external factors only.

C) Positive habits can lead to lasting happiness and well-being.

D) Happiness is solely determined by genetics and not influenced by habits.

5. How can individuals use neuroplasticity to overcome negative habits?

A) Neuroplasticity has no impact on negative habits.

B) By adopting new habits that are unrelated to happiness.

C) By consciously practicing positive habits to replace negative ones.

D) Overcoming negative habits is impossible due to the brain's fixed nature.

Answer: 1. (C) 2. (A) 3. (C) 4. (C) 5. (C)

****

Chapter 4: The External Influences on Happiness

"The happiness of your life depends upon the quality of your thoughts." - Marcus Aurelius

****

A Puzzle of Love and Perspective

In a quiet corner of their cozy home, a father sat engrossed in his newspaper, the rustling pages catching the sunlight streaming through the window. His thoughts were deep within the world of news and articles when a soft, innocent voice pierced through the tranquility.

"Papa, can you play with me?" the voice asked, carrying the hopes and desires of a young heart.

The father looked down to see his six-year-old child standing there, eyes wide with anticipation, a toy in hand. Though tempted by the invitation, his desire to stay informed and connected to the world via the newspaper was strong. He attempted to deflect the request, hoping to continue his reading.

But the child was persistent, determination shining in his eyes. "Papa, you should play with me," he insisted, his small voice resonating with a heartfelt plea.

Just as the father was about to deliver another gentle refusal, his gaze caught a full-page advertisement in the newspaper. It was an advertisement of an international courier company, displaying a world map. The map showcased their global reach, illustrating how they delivered goods to every corner of the world.

An idea sparked in the father's mind, a sudden stroke of brilliance that seemed tailor-made for this situation. He tore out the page with the world map, dividing it into numerous pieces, and scattered them across the floor. With a smile, he turned to the child and said, "Beta, this is your jigsaw puzzle. Assemble the world map properly, and once you're done, Papa will play with you."

Content with his inventive solution, the father returned to his newspaper, thinking he had bought himself some uninterrupted reading time. Little did he know that the child's cleverness would soon outshine his plan.

In the span of just a few minutes, the child called out with an excited voice, "Dad, look!" The father's attention shifted from the newspaper to the floor, where the world map lay perfectly assembled. He was utterly surprised, unable to fathom how his young child could solve such a complex puzzle so quickly.

Dumbfounded, the father asked, "How did you manage to do that so fast?"

The child's eyes twinkled with innocence, his response tinged with a mix of pride and honesty. "Papa, I have to confess... When you were tearing the newspaper, there was a face of a man on the other side. I don't know where New Zealand should be, where Canada should be, where India should be... But Papa, I know where the nose should be, where the forehead should be, where the eyes should be..."

The child's words resonated deeply with the father, his simple yet profound wisdom cutting through the complexities of geography. With a heartwarming realization, he understood that his child's perspective was not confined by borders and boundaries. The child had seen beyond the intricate lines on the map to the essence of a human being.

"Where the man was right, the world became right," the child concluded with a smile, capturing the essence of his innocence and reminding the father of the beauty in seeing the world through untainted eyes.

≈ ≈ ≈

External influences on happiness can significantly impact the overall well-being and level of happiness. These external factors interact with internal processes, including brain chemistry, habits, and cognitive functions, to shape a person's happiness and life satisfaction. Understanding these external influences is essential in creating environments and making choices that promote sustainable joy and well-being. Let's explore the external influences on happiness in detail:

1. Social Relationships:

- Strong social connections are one of the most significant external factors influencing happiness. Positive and supportive relationships with family, friends, romantic partners, and community members contribute to feelings of belonging, love, and support.

- Engaging in social activities and having a reliable support system can buffer against stress and adversity, leading to greater resilience and overall life satisfaction.

- Loneliness and social isolation, on the other hand, can have negative effects on mental health and well-being, leading to feelings of sadness, anxiety, and reduced quality of life.

2. Work and Career:

- Job satisfaction and fulfillment in one's career play a vital role in happiness. When you find meaning and purpose in your work, you experience a sense of accomplishment and personal growth.

- A positive work environment, supportive colleagues, and opportunities for growth and advancement contribute to job satisfaction and overall well-being.

- On the contrary, high levels of work-related stress, job insecurity, and lack of fulfillment can lead to decreased happiness and negative health outcomes.

3. Financial Situation:

- While money alone may not guarantee happiness, the financial situation can influence well-being to some extent. Having enough financial resources to meet basic needs and enjoy some discretionary spending can provide a sense of security and comfort.

- However, the pursuit of material wealth and the constant desire for more can lead to a phenomenon known as the **"hedonic treadmill,"** where you adapt to increases in wealth and constantly seek more without a lasting boost in happiness.

- Financial stress and struggles, such as debt or financial insecurity, can have significant negative effects on happiness and mental health.

4. Physical Health:

- Physical health is closely tied to happiness and well-being. Feeling physically well, having energy, and being free from chronic pain or illness contribute to overall life satisfaction.

- Engaging in regular exercise, maintaining a balanced diet, and getting sufficient sleep can positively impact mood and happiness.

- On the other hand, chronic health conditions or physical limitations can affect your emotional state and reduce overall life satisfaction.

5. Cultural and Societal Factors:

- Cultural norms, values, and societal expectations influence your perspectives on happiness and well-being. Different cultures prioritize various aspects of life that contribute to happiness, such as family, career success, community involvement, or spiritual fulfillment.

- Societal factors, such as income inequality, access to education, healthcare, and social support, also play a role in overall happiness levels.

6. Life Events and Adversity:

- Positive life events, such as getting married, having a child, or achieving a personal goal, can boost happiness temporarily. However, the **"hedonic treadmill"** effect suggests that you adapt to these changes, and the initial happiness boost subsides over time.

- Adverse life events, such as the loss of a loved one, illness, or significant stress, can lead to temporary decreases in happiness. However, you often demonstrate resilience and bounce back to your baseline level of well-being.

Building positive social connections, finding meaning in work, managing finances responsibly, prioritizing physical health, being mindful of cultural influences, and fostering resilience in the face of life challenges are all essential aspects of cultivating happiness and well-being.

A. Social Connections: The impact of relationships on joy.

Social connections and relationships have a profound impact on joy and overall well-being. Humans are social beings, and our ability to form and maintain meaningful relationships is essential for our emotional and mental health. Positive social connections provide a sense of belonging, love, support, and validation, all of which contribute to increased happiness and life satisfaction. Let's delve deeper into the impact of social connections on joy:

1. Sense of Belonging and Support:

- Social connections create a sense of belonging to a community or group, whether it's within a family, with friends, or in a larger social network. This feeling of belonging is fundamental to human happiness, as it fulfills the innate need for acceptance and inclusion.

- Supportive relationships offer emotional, practical, and psychological support during challenging times, reducing feelings of isolation and stress. Knowing that there are people who care and are there to help fosters a sense of security and well-being.

2. Emotional Resilience:

- Joyful relationships contribute to emotional resilience, enabling you to cope better with life's ups and downs. When faced with adversity, having supportive and caring individuals in one's life can provide comfort, encouragement, and a fresh perspective.

- Positive social connections can help mitigate the impact of stress and reduce the risk of developing mental health issues like anxiety and depression.

3. Happiness Contagion:

- The happiness of people we are connected to, can significantly influence our own happiness. Research has shown that happiness spreads through social networks, creating a phenomenon known as ***"happiness contagion."***

- When we are surrounded by happy and positive individuals, we are more likely to experience greater joy ourselves. This effect ripples through our social connections, extending the reach of happiness to others.

4. Social Support and Health:

- Social connections have a direct impact on physical health. Strong social support is associated with a reduced risk of developing chronic illnesses, improved immune function, and increased longevity.

- Joyful relationships encourage healthy behaviors, as individuals often engage in activities together, such as exercising, cooking nutritious meals, or participating in recreational pursuits.

5. Shared Experiences and Memories:

- Joyful relationships offer opportunities for shared experiences and the creation of positive memories. Engaging in enjoyable activities with loved ones enhances the joy and satisfaction derived from those experiences.

- Fond memories of shared moments can be a source of happiness during difficult times and contribute to a sense of gratitude for the meaningful relationships in one's life.

6. Brain Chemistry and Social Bonding:

- Social connections trigger the release of oxytocin, often referred to as the **"bonding hormone" or "love hormone." Oxytocin** fosters feelings of trust, connection, and affection, deepening the emotional bond between individuals.

- The release of oxytocin during positive social interactions contributes to feelings of happiness and reinforces the desire to maintain and strengthen these relationships.

7. Reducing Feelings of Loneliness:

- Loneliness can have a detrimental impact on happiness and well-being. Positive social connections act as a protective factor against loneliness, providing a sense of companionship and reducing feelings of isolation.

- For individuals experiencing loneliness, developing and nurturing social connections can lead to significant improvements in overall happiness and life satisfaction.

Cultivating and cherishing meaningful relationships enriches our lives and creates a positive feedback loop of happiness and well-being. Prioritizing social connections and nurturing healthy, joyful relationships is a key aspect of leading a fulfilling and happy life.

B. The Influence of Environment: Creating a happy space.

The environment in which we live and spend our time has a significant influence on our well-being and happiness. Creating a happy space involves intentionally shaping our physical surroundings, social interactions, and daily routines to promote positive emotions, relaxation, and joy. Let's explore in detail how the environment affects our happiness and how we can design a happy space:

1. Physical Environment:

- **Natural Elements:** Incorporating natural elements like **plants, sunlight, and views of nature** can have a calming and uplifting effect on our mood. Exposure to nature has been linked to reduced stress and increased feelings of happiness.

- **Organized and Clutter-Free Space:** A clutter-free and organized living space promotes a sense of calm and reduces feelings of overwhelm. Keeping the environment tidy and free from unnecessary clutter can positively impact our mental well-being.

- **Personal Touch:** Surrounding ourselves with objects and decor that hold sentimental value or represent our interests and passions can create a sense of identity and comfort.

- **Colors and Lighting:** Colors can evoke different emotions, and choosing a color scheme that aligns with positive feelings can contribute to a happy atmosphere. Additionally, ample natural lighting can enhance mood and energy levels.

2. Social Environment:

- **Supportive Relationships:** Surrounding ourselves with supportive and positive individuals fosters a sense of belonging and emotional well-being. Building and maintaining healthy social connections are essential for happiness.

- **Social Activities:** Engaging in social activities that bring joy, laughter, and shared experiences can strengthen social bonds and contribute to overall happiness.

- Boundaries: Setting healthy boundaries in our social interactions can help reduce stress and create a harmonious social environment.

3. Daily Routines and Habits:

- **Morning Rituals:** Starting the day with a positive morning routine, such as practicing gratitude, meditating, or engaging in physical activity, can set a positive tone for the rest of the day.

- **Mindful Breaks:** Incorporating mindful breaks throughout the day, even for a few minutes, can provide moments of relaxation and mental rejuvenation.

- **Sleep and Rest:** Prioritizing adequate and restful sleep is crucial for maintaining a positive mood and overall well-being.

4. Work Environment:

- Designing a comfortable and inspiring workspace can positively impact productivity, creativity, and job satisfaction.

- Creating a positive work culture that values collaboration, appreciation, and work-life balance can contribute to a happier work environment.

5. Minimizing Negative Influences:

- Limiting exposure to negative news, social media, or toxic relationships can prevent unnecessary stress and anxiety.

- Being mindful of the media we consume and curating our social media feeds to include positive and uplifting content can help maintain a happy mental space.

6. Emotional Safety:

- Feeling emotionally safe in our environment, where we can express ourselves authentically without fear of judgment, fosters a sense of well-being and happiness.

- Surrounding ourselves with individuals who respect and validate our emotions can contribute to a positive emotional climate.

7. Cultivating Gratitude:

- Practicing gratitude for the things we have in our environment and the positive experiences we encounter can enhance feelings of contentment and joy.

- Keeping a ***gratitude journal*** or regularly expressing appreciation for the people and things around us reinforces positive emotions.

Mindful morning and daily routines, along with a positive work culture, enhance overall well-being. By minimizing negative influences, practicing gratitude, and prioritizing emotional safety, we can create a happy space that promotes sustainable joy and happiness in our lives.

C. Pursuit of Meaning and Purpose: The role of passion and fulfillment.

The pursuit of meaning and purpose is a fundamental aspect of human well-being and happiness. When you engage in activities that align with your passions and provide a sense of fulfillment, you experience a deeper sense of satisfaction and joy in your life. Understanding the role of passion and fulfillment in the pursuit of meaning and purpose is essential for cultivating lasting happiness. Let's explore this concept in detail:

1. Passion and Intrinsic Motivation:

- Passion refers to a strong and compelling interest or enthusiasm for a particular activity, hobby, or pursuit. It is characterized by an internal drive and intrinsic motivation to engage in the activity for its own sake, rather than for external rewards.

- When you pursue activities you are passionate about, you experience a sense of joy, flow, and deep engagement. Time seems to pass quickly, and you feel fully absorbed in the present moment.

- Pursuing your passions can lead to a state of **"intrinsic happiness,"** where the activity itself becomes a source of joy and fulfillment.

2. Alignment with Values and Beliefs:

- The pursuit of meaning and purpose is often connected to an alignment with one's values and beliefs. Engaging in activities that are in harmony with our ***core values*** gives life a deeper sense of significance and authenticity.

- When you live in alignment with your values, you experience a sense of fulfillment and a greater sense of purpose in your actions.

3. Contributing to Others and the Greater Good:

- Finding meaning and purpose often involves contributing to something greater than oneself, such as helping others, making a positive impact on the community, or working towards a larger societal goal.

- Acts of kindness, volunteering, or engaging in philanthropic activities can generate a profound sense of fulfillment and joy by providing a sense of purpose and contribution to the well-being of others.

4. Personal Growth and Mastery:

- Pursuing activities that challenge you to grow and develop your skills can lead to a sense of mastery and accomplishment.

- The process of learning and improving in an area of interest can bring a sense of satisfaction and fulfillment, contributing to overall happiness.

5. Resilience in the Face of Challenges:

- Pursuing meaning and purpose can provide individuals with a sense of direction and resilience during challenging times.

- When you have a strong sense of purpose, you are more likely to navigate obstacles and setbacks with greater determination and optimism.

6. Connection to Identity and Self-Expression:

- Engaging in activities that align with personal interests and talents can enhance self-expression and foster a strong sense of identity.

- When you are able to express yourself authentically through your pursuits, you experience a deeper sense of fulfillment and happiness.

7. Balancing Passion and Realistic Goals:

- While passion is essential for a sense of purpose, it is important to strike a balance between pursuing what you love and setting realistic goals.

- Some passions may not be viable as full-time careers, but finding ways to incorporate them into your life, even as hobbies or side projects, can still contribute to happiness and fulfillment.

Passion and intrinsic motivation propel you towards activities that bring joy, fulfillment, and a sense of purpose. Engaging in pursuits aligned with personal values, contributing to others, fostering personal growth, and expressing one's authentic self all play crucial roles in cultivating happiness. Balancing passion with realistic goals allows you to incorporate meaningful activities into your life, contributing to sustainable joy and a greater sense of fulfillment.

QUIZ TIME

1. What is the primary focus of, "External Influences on Happiness"?

A) Examining the impact of internal factors on happiness.

B) Analyzing the role of brain chemistry in social relationships.

C) Understanding the influence of external factors on happiness and well-being.

D) Exploring the connection between habits and external environments.

2. How do social connections impact an individual's happiness?

A) Social connections have no impact on happiness.

B) Social connections can lead to increased stress and anxiety.

C) Positive social connections are strongly linked to higher levels of happiness.

D) Social connections solely affect external behaviors, not happiness.

3. What is the significance of the environment in influencing happiness?

A) The environment has no impact on an individual's well-being.

B) The environment is solely determined by genetics and cannot be changed.

C) A positive environment can contribute to greater happiness and life satisfaction.

D) The environment only affects physical health, not emotional experiences.

4. How can individuals create a happier environment in their daily lives?

A) By solely focusing on individual happiness without considering external factors.

B) By surrounding themselves with material possessions.

C) By cultivating positive relationships and fostering a supportive community.

D) Creating a happier environment is impossible due to external circumstances.

5. What role does the pursuit of meaning and purpose play in enhancing happiness?

A) Pursuit of meaning and purpose has no impact on happiness.

B) Pursuit of meaning and purpose leads to decreased happiness.

C) Finding meaning and purpose in life contributes to greater overall well-being and happiness.

D) Pursuit of meaning and purpose solely applies to external achievements.

Answers: All (C)

****

Chapter 5: Amplifying Serotonin Naturally

"The human brain is the most powerful tool you can possibly possess." - Bill Nye

****

The Pursuit of Happiness: A Tale of Self-Discovery

In a village surrounded by mountains and the sea, there lived a simple stone cutter named Takumi. Day after day, he diligently cut stones from the Mountainside, feeling skilled yet discontent with his life. One hot day, Takumi saw a wealthy merchant pass by in a fancy carriage with servants and treasures all around. Takumi thought, "If only I could be as wealthy as that merchant, I'd be happy." Unexpectedly, a mysterious voice whispered, "Your wish shall be granted."

In a flash, Takumi transformed into the wealthy merchant, living in a luxurious mansion with servants attending to his needs. Initially, he was ecstatic, but he soon realized the sun's heat still made him uncomfortable. As Takumi considered his situation, he saw the sun shining brightly and thought, "The sun is more powerful than any merchant. If only I could be the sun, I'd be happy." The voice whispered again, "Your wish shall be granted."

And just like that, Takumi became the sun, enjoying warming the Earth and controlling the seasons. However, he soon found that clouds could block his light and power. Annoyed, he thought, "The clouds are more powerful than the sun. If only I could be a cloud, I'd be happy." The voice obliged, and Takumi transformed into a massive cloud.

As a cloud, Takumi felt mighty, casting shadows below and releasing heavy rain. But one day, he noticed a large boulder on the Mountainside unaffected by rain and wind. He thought, "The stone is more powerful than the clouds. If only I could be a stone, I'd be happy." The voice granted his wish, and Takumi became a large boulder, now feeling indestructible.

Takumi was soon disturbed by the rhythmic tapping of a stonecutter's chisel. The stonecutter was slowly chipping away at the boulder, reducing its size. Takumi realized that even a mighty stone could be shaped by a simple stonecutter. He wished, "If only I could be a stonecutter, then I would be happy." The mysterious voice granted his wish once more, and Takumi returned to being a humble stonecutter.

And so, Takumi returned to his life as a stonecutter. Through his experiences, he gained insight into the true meaning of happiness. No longer envious of others, he came to appreciate the significance of his own work, his life, and his unique abilities. As you journey through your own life, remember Takumi's lesson. It's a lesson that's as relevant today as it was when the story was first told centuries ago.

You see, we often think that happiness lies in external things – in money, power, or fame. Just like Takumi, we believe that if we had more of these things, we would be happy. But the truth is that happiness is an inside job – a state of mind, a way of being. It's not something that can be acquired, but something that can be cultivated. And the good news is that we can cultivate happiness regardless of our external circumstances.

We can find happiness in the simple things of life – in the warmth of the sun on our skin, in the beauty of a sunset, and in the smiles of loved ones. We can find happiness in the work that we do, in the people we serve, and in the difference we make in the world. *We don't have to be wealthy, powerful, or famous to be happy. We just have to be ourselves, doing what we love, with the people we love.*

But perhaps the most important lesson that Takumi teaches us is that *happiness is not a destination, but a journey*. It's not something that we arrive at, but something that we constantly strive for. Happiness is not a fixed state, but a dynamic one. It's something that we have to work at every day – through small acts of kindness, moments of gratitude, and a deep sense of purpose.

So as you go about your day, remember that happiness is within your reach. It's not something that you have to chase or acquire, but something that you can cultivate within yourself. Remember the story of Takumi, the stone cutter, and let it remind you that *true happiness lies within you*. It's up to you to find it, nurture it, and share it with the world.

≈ ≈ ≈

Understanding the importance of serotonin in happiness can help you make lifestyle choices that support its production and contribute to overall mental health and happiness. However, it's essential to recognize that serotonin is just one of many neurotransmitters and factors that influence happiness, and maintaining well-being involves a holistic approach that includes other elements like social connections, meaningful activities, and self-care.

A. Understanding Serotonin's Role in Happiness.

Serotonin is a neurotransmitter that plays a vital role in regulating mood, emotions, and overall well-being. It is often referred to as the **"happy chemical"** due to its association with positive emotions and happiness. Understanding serotonin's role in happiness involves exploring its functions in the brain and how it influences various aspects of our emotional and mental states. Here's a detailed explanation of serotonin's role in happiness:

1. Neurotransmitter and Brain Function:

- Serotonin is a neurotransmitter, which means it is a chemical messenger that facilitates communication between nerve cells (neurons) in the brain.

- Neurons release serotonin into synapses, the gaps between neurons, where it binds to specific receptors on neighboring neurons. This binding process influences the electrical activity and transmission of signals between neurons.

- Serotonin is produced in the brain and some parts of the gastrointestinal tract (the gut-brain axis), and its levels can fluctuate based on various internal and external factors.

2. Mood Regulation:

- One of serotonin's primary roles is mood regulation. It helps modulate and stabilize emotions, influencing feelings of happiness, contentment, and well-being.

- Adequate serotonin levels are associated with positive emotions, while low levels have been linked to conditions like depression and anxiety.

- Serotonin contributes to a balanced emotional state, allowing individuals to experience a range of emotions without being overwhelmed by negative feelings.

3. Stress and Anxiety:

- Serotonin plays a role in regulating the body's stress response. It helps dampen the activity of the amygdala, a brain region involved in processing fear and stress.

- When serotonin levels are sufficient, it can help reduce the impact of stress and anxiety, making it easier for individuals to cope with challenging situations.

4. Sleep and Circadian Rhythm:

- Serotonin is involved in regulating sleep-wake cycles and the body's internal clock **(circadian rhythm).**

- Adequate serotonin levels contribute to restful sleep and healthy sleep patterns. Disruptions in serotonin function can lead to sleep disturbances and insomnia.

5. Social Behavior and Bonding:

- Serotonin influences social behavior and plays a role in forming and maintaining social bonds.

- Higher serotonin levels are associated with increased feelings of trust, empathy, and connectedness with others.

6. Appetite and Satiety:

- Serotonin is involved in regulating appetite and satiety (feeling full after eating).

- It helps signal the brain when the body has consumed enough food, promoting a sense of satisfaction and reducing the desire to eat further.

7. Reward and Pleasure:

- Serotonin is part of the brain's reward system and is involved in the experience of pleasure and reward.

- Adequate serotonin levels contribute to a sense of reward and positive reinforcement when engaging in enjoyable activities.

8. Emotional Resilience:

- Serotonin is believed to play a role in emotional resilience, helping individuals cope with stress and adversity.
- Higher serotonin levels are associated with better emotional regulation and the ability to bounce back from negative experiences.

B. Lifestyle Strategies to Increase Serotonin Levels.

Lifestyle strategies can significantly impact serotonin levels in the brain, promoting positive mood and overall well-being. These strategies focus on activities and habits that support serotonin production, release, and receptor sensitivity. By incorporating these practices into daily life, you can naturally increase serotonin levels and experience enhanced happiness and emotional resilience. Here are some lifestyle strategies to increase serotonin levels in detail:

1. Regular Exercise:

- Engaging in regular physical activity, especially aerobic exercises like jogging, cycling, swimming, or dancing, can boost serotonin levels.

- Exercise increases the availability of tryptophan, an amino acid used to produce serotonin, in the brain.

- It also triggers the release of endorphins, which interact with serotonin receptors to enhance feelings of pleasure and well-being.

2. Exposure to Natural Light:

- Sunlight exposure has a positive impact on serotonin production and release. Spending time outdoors during daylight hours can elevate serotonin levels in the brain.

- Sunlight also influences the body's production of vitamin D, which is linked to improved mood and increased serotonin synthesis.

3. Balanced Diet:

- Consuming a well-balanced diet that includes foods rich in tryptophan can support serotonin production.
- Foods such as turkey, chicken, fish, eggs, nuts, seeds, and dairy products are good sources of tryptophan.

- Additionally, incorporating complex carbohydrates like whole grains and fruits can help facilitate tryptophan absorption in the brain.

4. Mindfulness and Meditation:

- Mindfulness practices and meditation techniques can reduce stress and increase serotonin levels.

- Mindfulness helps regulate the amygdala, the brain's fear center, and reduces the stress response, leading to higher serotonin activity.

5. Social Connections:

- Positive social interactions and nurturing relationships contribute to increased serotonin levels.

- Engaging in meaningful social activities, spending time with loved ones, and building a supportive social network all support serotonin release.

6. Acts of Kindness:

- Engaging in acts of kindness and helping others can boost serotonin levels and generate feelings of fulfillment and happiness.

- Volunteering or performing random acts of kindness has been linked to increased serotonin production.

7. Regular Sleep:

- Adequate and restful sleep is crucial for maintaining healthy serotonin levels and overall mental well-being.

- Disrupted sleep patterns or sleep deprivation can negatively affect serotonin production and lead to mood disturbances.

8. Creative Expression:

- Engaging in creative activities, such as art, music, writing, or crafting, can stimulate the brain and contribute to increased serotonin levels.

- Creative expression can foster a sense of accomplishment and joy, supporting overall mental health.

9. Limiting Stress:

- Chronic stress can deplete serotonin levels over time. Engaging in stress-reducing practices, such as yoga, deep breathing exercises, or spending time in nature, can help maintain healthy serotonin levels.

Lifestyle strategies play a vital role in increasing serotonin levels naturally. Regular exercise, exposure to natural light, a balanced diet, mindfulness and meditation, positive social connections, acts of kindness, regular sleep, creative expression, and stress reduction all support serotonin production and release.

C. Cognitive Techniques for Boosting Serotonin.

Cognitive techniques are powerful mental strategies that can help boost serotonin levels and promote a positive and optimistic outlook on life. These techniques focus on changing thought patterns, beliefs, and behaviors to foster a more constructive and content mindset. By actively engaging in cognitive techniques, you can rewire your brain to support increased serotonin production and release. Here are some cognitive techniques for boosting serotonin:

1. Positive Affirmations:

- Positive affirmations involve repeating positive and uplifting statements to oneself. These statements can focus on self-worth, capabilities, and positive traits.
- Regularly practicing positive affirmations can help rewire the brain to focus on positive aspects of life, leading to increased feelings of self-confidence and well-being.

2. Gratitude Practice:

- Practicing gratitude involves consciously acknowledging and appreciating the positive aspects of life, both big and small.

- Keeping a **gratitude journal** or simply taking a few moments each day to reflect on things to be grateful for can increase feelings of contentment and happiness.

3. Reframing Negative Thoughts:

- Reframing involves consciously changing negative or unhelpful thoughts into more positive and constructive ones.

- By challenging negative thought patterns and replacing them with more balanced and optimistic perspectives, individuals can reduce anxiety and promote a more positive mindset.

4. Mindfulness Meditation:

- Mindfulness meditation involves being present in the moment, observing thoughts and emotions without judgment.

- Regular mindfulness practice can reduce stress, improve emotional regulation, and increase self-awareness, all of which contribute to increased serotonin levels.

5. Visualization:

- Visualization techniques involve mentally imagining positive and joyful experiences.

- By regularly engaging in positive visualization, individuals can activate the brain's reward pathways, leading to an increase in serotonin production.

6. Cognitive Behavioral Therapy (CBT):

- CBT is a structured therapeutic approach that helps individuals identify and change negative thought patterns and behaviors.

- CBT has been shown to be effective in treating depression and anxiety, and it can contribute to increased serotonin activity in the brain.

7. Self-Compassion:

- Practicing self-compassion involves treating oneself with kindness and understanding, especially during challenging times.

- Being self-compassionate can lead to reduced feelings of self-criticism and increased emotional resilience.

8. Positive Social Interactions:

- Engaging in positive social interactions and surrounding oneself with supportive and uplifting individuals can boost serotonin levels.

- Positive social connections promote feelings of belonging and contribute to a sense of happiness and well-being.

9. Setting and Achieving Goals:

- Working towards meaningful goals and celebrating achievements can stimulate the brain's reward system and increase serotonin levels.

- Setting realistic and attainable goals provides a sense of purpose and fulfillment.

By incorporating these cognitive techniques into daily life, you can foster a more positive and constructive mindset, leading to increased serotonin activity in the brain. Over time, these techniques can become habits, creating lasting changes in thought patterns and emotional responses

QUIZ TIME

1. What is the role of serotonin in happiness?

a) It has no impact on happiness

b) It contributes to feelings of well-being and happiness

c) It only affects negative emotions

d) It controls physical health

2. Which foods are known to naturally boost serotonin levels?

a) Sugary snacks and drinks

b) High-protein foods

c) Processed foods

d) Fruits and vegetables

3. How does regular exercise influence serotonin levels?

a) It decreases serotonin levels

b) It has no impact on serotonin

c) It increases serotonin production and release

d) It only affects dopamine levels

4. What benefit does exposure to sunlight provide for serotonin levels?

a) It has no effect on serotonin

b) It decreases serotonin production

c) It triggers the release of serotonin

d) It only affects melatonin levels

5. How can mindfulness and meditation contribute to increased serotonin?

a) They have no impact on serotonin

b) They decrease serotonin levels

c) They increase brain activity but not serotonin

d) They enhance serotonin production and receptor sensitivity

Answers: 1. (b) 2. (b) 3. (c) 4. (c) 5. (d)

****

Chapter 6: Boosting Dopamine for Lasting Joy

"The mind is everything. What you think, you become." - Buddha

****

Feathers of Contentment: A Raven's Journey

Once upon a time, a raven was deeply discontent with its life. One day, perched upon a tree branch, tears streamed down its feathers. Nearby, a monk meditated on the tree. A tear fell upon the monk's cheek, catching his attention. Looking up, he saw the distraught raven.

With kindness, the monk inquired, "Why do you weep, my friend?" The raven poured out its heart, lamenting how unloved and unwanted it felt, yearning for a life better than its own. The monk, his heart stirred with compassion, gently advised, "We must find contentment in our circumstances."

Yet, the raven remained unconvinced, and its tears persisted. Undeterred, the monk suggested, "Share your desires with me. Through my mantra, I can grant your wish." The raven's spirits lifted, and it eagerly expressed its desire to become a swan, believing such transformation would bring happiness.

The monk agreed, but he proposed a condition: first, the raven should seek out a swan and determine if it's truly content. As the raven soared off, the monk waited, contemplating the bird's lesson.

Approaching a swan swimming in a serene pond, the raven marveled at its beauty. Assuming the swan must be the happiest creature, it complimented the swan's radiance. Yet, the swan confided its own discontent, lamenting its lack of vibrant colors and envying the parrot's brilliance.

Following the raven's curiosity, it journeyed to the parrot, envying its vivid hues. The parrot, however, disclosed its unease, fearing the confinement of a cage.

Convinced that the peacock, resplendent and magnificent, must be the happiest, the raven sought it out. To its surprise, the peacock bemoaned its captivity and the pain of its stolen feathers.

Finally understanding, the raven returned to the monk and related its discoveries. The monk's wisdom shone as he explained that true contentment comes from within. The raven, now enlightened, embraced its raven identity. It realized that happiness isn't found in external appearances or comparisons, but in being satisfied with oneself.

In sharing this story, we reflect on our own lives. Often, we measure ourselves against others, leading to dissatisfaction and sorrow. Yet, true happiness springs from appreciating what we have. If we free ourselves from the cycle of comparison, we can find contentment in our uniqueness. Just as the raven learned, the one who is content with their own blessings is truly the happiest of all. Buddha's wisdom resonates through this tale, reminding us to keep smiling and cherish what we possess.

≈ ≈ ≈

Boosting dopamine levels is essential for experiencing lasting joy and a sense of reward and fulfillment in life. Dopamine is a neurotransmitter that plays a crucial role in the **brain's reward system**. It is associated with feelings of pleasure, motivation, and reinforcement. However, it's important to approach dopamine enhancement in a balanced and healthy way, as excessive dopamine activation can lead to addictive behaviors and negative consequences.

A. The Role of Dopamine in Reward and Pleasure.

Dopamine is a neurotransmitter that plays a central role in the **brain's reward and pleasure system**. It is a chemical messenger that helps transmit signals between **neurons (nerve cells)** in various regions of the brain. Dopamine is involved in a wide range of physiological and psychological functions, but its role in the reward and pleasure pathways is particularly significant. Here's a detailed explanation of the role of dopamine in reward and pleasure:

1. Role in Pleasure and Reinforcement:

- Dopamine is often referred to as the **"feel-good" neurotransmitter** because it is associated with feelings of pleasure, reward, and reinforcement.

- When dopamine, creates a sense of pleasure and positive reinforcement, motivating individuals to seek out and repeat the behavior or activity that triggered the dopamine release.

- This reinforcement mechanism is fundamental for survival, as it encourages behaviors that promote well-being, such as eating, socializing, and reproducing.

2. Motivation and Goal-Directed Behavior:

- Dopamine plays a crucial role in motivation and goal-directed behavior. When we set goals and work towards achieving them, the anticipation and pursuit of rewards lead to dopamine release.

- As we make progress towards our goals and experience success, dopamine release reinforces our behavior, increasing our motivation to continue working towards those goals.

3. Learning and Adaptation:

- Dopamine also plays a role in learning and adaptation. It helps the brain recognize and remember which behaviors or experiences are rewarding or pleasurable.

- When dopamine is released during a positive experience, the brain strengthens the connections between the neurons involved, making it more likely that the behavior will be repeated in the future.

4. Addiction and Substance Abuse:

- The role of dopamine in the reward pathway also explains its involvement in addiction and substance abuse.

- Drugs and certain addictive behaviors, such as gambling or gaming, can lead to abnormally high levels of dopamine release, creating an intense and artificial sense of pleasure.

- Over time, the brain adapts to these high dopamine levels by reducing dopamine receptor sensitivity, leading to tolerance and dependence on the addictive substance or behavior.

5. Role in Mood and Emotions:

- Dopamine is not only involved in pleasure and reward but also plays a role in mood and emotions.

- Imbalances in dopamine levels have been linked to various mood disorders, such as depression and bipolar disorder.

Dopamine plays a critical role in the brain's reward and pleasure system. It is associated with feelings of pleasure and reinforcement, motivating us to seek out rewarding experiences and pursue our goals. Dopamine also plays a role in learning and adaptation, helping the brain recognize and remember rewarding behaviors. However, it's important to note that dopamine is just one of many neurotransmitters and systems involved in complex behaviors and emotions.

B. Healthy Dopamine-Boosting Habits.

Boosting dopamine levels through healthy habits can contribute to overall well-being and a sense of reward and fulfillment. It's essential to approach dopamine enhancement in a balanced way to avoid excessive stimulation or negative consequences. Here are some healthy dopamine-boosting habits explained in detail:

1. Regular Exercise:

- Engaging in regular physical activity, especially aerobic exercises like jogging, cycling, or dancing, can boost dopamine production and release.

- Exercise triggers the release of endorphins, which interact with dopamine receptors, leading to feelings of pleasure and improved mood.

- Regular exercise also increases the sensitivity of dopamine receptors, making them more responsive to the neurotransmitter.

2. Balanced Nutrition:

- Consuming a balanced diet that includes adequate protein, healthy fats, and essential nutrients supports dopamine production.

- Foods rich in **tyrosine**, an amino acid precursor to dopamine, can be beneficial. Such foods include lean meats, eggs, fish, nuts, and seeds.

- ***Avoid excessive consumption of sugary and processed foods***, as they can lead to fluctuations in blood sugar levels and negatively impact dopamine regulation.

3. Mindfulness and Meditation:

- Mindfulness practices and meditation have been shown to increase dopamine receptor sensitivity in the brain.

- Practicing mindfulness allows individuals to savor positive experiences and cultivate gratitude, which can contribute to enhanced dopamine release.

4. Goal Setting and Achievement:

- Setting meaningful goals and working towards their achievement can trigger dopamine release.

- Breaking down larger goals into smaller, achievable tasks and celebrating each milestone can sustain dopamine levels over time.

5. Social Connections and Positive Relationships:

- Positive social interactions and spending time with loved ones can lead to dopamine release.

- Cultivating supportive and meaningful relationships provides a sense of connection and belonging, which enhances well-being.

6. Novelty and Exploration:

- Novel experiences and exploration activate the brain's reward system, leading to dopamine release.

- Trying new activities, traveling to new places, or learning new skills can stimulate the brain and promote a sense of reward and excitement.

7. Acts of Kindness and Altruism:

- Engaging in acts of kindness and helping others can trigger dopamine release and lead to feelings of fulfillment and happiness.

- Volunteer work and contributing to the community are examples of activities that can boost dopamine levels.

8. Healthy Stress Management:

- Chronic stress can negatively affect dopamine regulation. Adopting healthy stress management techniques, such as yoga, meditation, or spending time in nature, can help maintain balanced dopamine levels.

9. Sufficient Sleep:

- Adequate and restful sleep is crucial for maintaining optimal dopamine levels and overall brain health.

- Disrupted sleep patterns or sleep deprivation can negatively impact dopamine production and lead to mood disturbances.

10. Limiting Excessive Stimulation:

- While seeking enjoyable activities and experiences is beneficial, it's essential to avoid excessive stimulation or reliance on external rewards.

- Overindulgence in addictive substances or behaviors can lead to negative consequences and disrupt dopamine regulation.

Adopting healthy habits that naturally boost dopamine can contribute to lasting joy and a sense of reward in life. Regular exercise, balanced nutrition, mindfulness and meditation, goal setting, positive social connections, novelty, acts of kindness, stress management, sufficient sleep, and moderation in stimulation are all essential for maintaining balanced dopamine levels.

By incorporating these habits into your daily life, you can enhance your overall well-being and cultivate a greater sense of happiness and fulfillment. It's important to remember that everyone's dopamine response is unique, and seeking a balanced approach to well-being is key to sustaining lasting joy.

C. Nurturing Activities to Increase Dopamine Levels.

Engaging in nurturing activities can naturally boost dopamine levels and promote feelings of pleasure, reward, and well-being. These activities provide positive stimulation for the brain's reward system, leading to the release of dopamine. Dopamine is associated with motivation, positive reinforcement, and the anticipation of pleasure, making nurturing activities essential for maintaining overall happiness and mental health. Here's a detailed explanation of nurturing activities that can increase dopamine levels:

1. Exercise and Physical Activity:

- Regular aerobic exercise, such as running, swimming, or dancing, increases dopamine production and receptor sensitivity.

- Exercise triggers the release of endorphins and other neurotransmitters, contributing to the feelings of joy and satisfaction.

- Engaging in enjoyable physical activities can further enhance the rewarding effects and motivation to continue being active.

2. Creative Pursuits:

- Activities that tap into your creativity, such as painting, writing, or playing a musical instrument, can elevate dopamine levels.

- The process of creation and the sense of accomplishment from expressing yourself artistically contribute to increased dopamine release.

3. Social Interaction:

- Positive social interactions, such as spending time with friends, family, or loved ones, trigger dopamine release.

- Meaningful connections and shared experiences foster feelings of pleasure, belonging, and reward.

4. Acts of Kindness and Altruism:

- Engaging in acts of kindness or helping others in need can lead to increased dopamine levels.

- Altruistic behavior triggers the brain's reward system, promoting positive emotions and a sense of fulfillment.

5. Goal Achievement:

- Progressing towards and achieving goals activates the brain's reward pathways and boosts dopamine release.

- Celebrating milestones and accomplishments reinforces positive behavior and enhances motivation.

6. Mindfulness and Meditation:

- Mindfulness practices, such as meditation, promote increased dopamine receptor sensitivity in the brain.
- Being present in the moment and cultivating gratitude contribute to a sense of reward and contentment.

7. Spending Time in Nature:

- Being in natural environments and engaging with nature can elevate dopamine levels.

- Activities like hiking, gardening, or simply spending time outdoors provide a sense of joy and rejuvenation.

8. Learning and Intellectual Stimulation:

- Engaging in intellectually stimulating activities, such as reading, learning new skills, or solving puzzles, can increase dopamine release.

- Curiosity and the pursuit of knowledge are rewarding experiences for the brain.

9. Laughter and Humor:

- Laughter triggers dopamine release and is associated with positive emotions and pleasure.

- Engage in activities that make you laugh, such as watching a comedy show or spending time with humorous friends.

10. Music and Dancing:

- Listening to music and dancing can lead to increased dopamine production and a sense of enjoyment.
- Music with emotional resonance can evoke powerful positive feelings.

It's important to note that the impact of nurturing activities on dopamine levels can vary from person to person. What brings pleasure and reward to one individual may differ for another. It's essential to explore and incorporate activities that align with your interests, values, and preferences. Balancing different nurturing activities in your life can provide a diverse range of rewards and foster a greater sense of happiness and fulfillment. Embracing these activities regularly can help maintain a positive mood, boost motivation, and contribute to a more rewarding and enriching life.

QUIZ TIME

1. What role does dopamine play in the brain?

a) It only regulates body temperature

b) It is responsible for vision

c) It plays a role in reward and pleasure

d) It controls lung function

2. How does setting and achieving goals impact dopamine levels?

a) It has no effect on dopamine

b) It decreases dopamine production

c) It triggers dopamine release, motivating further progress

d) It only affects serotonin levels

3. Why is celebrating progress important for dopamine levels?

a) It has no connection to dopamine

b) It decreases dopamine production

c) It promotes the release of serotonin

d) It reinforces positive behaviors and increases dopamine release

4. How do creative pursuits affect dopamine levels?

a) They have no impact on dopamine

b) They decrease dopamine production

c) They stimulate dopamine release and enhance mood

d) They only affect oxytocin levels

5. How do positive experiences contribute to dopamine levels?

a) They have no impact on dopamine

b) They decrease dopamine production

c) They trigger dopamine release, fostering a sense of reward

d) They only affect endorphin levels

Answers: 1. (c) 2. (c) 3 (d) 4. (c) 5. (c)

****

Chapter 7: Fostering Oxytocin for Connection and Well-being

"Happiness is not a destination; it is a way of life." – Girendra Nath Singh

****

The 99 Club: A Tale of Chasing Happiness

Once upon a time, there was a king who went for a walk with his advisor. They came across a farm where a happy family lived - a dad, a mom, and their son. The family was full of life, always smiling and singing together.

The king looked at them and said, "I live in a big palace with everything I need, but these people seem even happier than me. Why is that?"

The advisor replied, "Well, they're not part of the 99 Club."

Confused, the king asked, "What's the 99 Club?"

The advisor explained, "If you give me 99 gold coins, I'll tell you about it in six months."

The king agreed and gave the advisor the coins. The advisor secretly put the coins at the family's doorstep. The next morning, the family found the coins and were excited. They counted them and saw there were 99.

But they wanted an even 100 coins, so they worked hard to get that last one. While they were doing this, the mom took two coins and went shopping. This upset the dad, and he got angry.

Every day, the dad would count the coins, and one day he saw there were only 97 left. He found out his wife and son had spent some coins, and he got even more upset.

Six months later, the king and advisor came back to the farm. The family was no longer happy. They argued a lot and had lost their joy.

The king asked, "What happened? Why are they so different now?"

The advisor explained, "They're in the 99 Club now."

Perplexed, the king asked, **"What's the 99 Club?"**

The advisor clarified, **"It's when you have 99 coins but keep chasing after one more, you forget to enjoy the 99 you already have."**

The advisor taught the king an important lesson: ***Happiness isn't about waiting for something more. It's about enjoying what you have now and finding joy in the journey, not just the destination.***

≈≈≈

Oxytocin plays a central role in social bonding and happiness. Its release during positive social interactions fosters emotional connections, trust, empathy, and feelings of happiness and contentment. Oxytocin promotes a sense of security and belonging in relationships and enhances overall well-being. By nurturing positive social interactions and meaningful relationships, you can experience the positive effects of oxytocin, leading to a more fulfilling and happier life. Let us explore it further:

A. Oxytocin's Impact on Social Bonding and Happiness.

Oxytocin is a neuro hormone that plays a crucial role in social bonding and happiness. It is often referred to as the **"love hormone" or "bonding hormone"** because of its association with positive social interactions and emotional connections. Oxytocin is produced in **the hypothalamus**, a region of the brain, and is released into the bloodstream and brain in response to various social and emotional stimuli. Here's a detailed explanation of oxytocin's impact on social bonding and happiness:

1. Social Bonding:

- Oxytocin is released during moments of positive social interactions, particularly those that involve physical affection, such as hugging, cuddling, and touching.

- It fosters feelings of trust and intimacy between individuals, strengthening emotional bonds in various relationships, including romantic partners, family members, and friends.

- Oxytocin promotes attachment and the desire to nurture and protect loved ones, which is essential for building and maintaining healthy relationships.

- During social bonding, oxytocin acts as a **"social glue,"** enhancing emotional connections and reinforcing positive social behavior.

2. Enhanced Empathy and Social Perception:

- Oxytocin enhances empathy, making individuals more sensitive and attuned to others' emotions and needs.

- It improves the ability to accurately interpret social cues and facial expressions, leading to better social perception and understanding.

- This heightened empathy fosters deeper emotional connections with others and facilitates more meaningful interactions.

3. Stress Reduction:

- Oxytocin acts as a natural stress reducer by dampening the activity of the stress hormone cortisol.

- Positive social interactions that trigger oxytocin release can help alleviate feelings of stress and anxiety, leading to a sense of relaxation and well-being.

4. Positive Mood and Happiness:

- Oxytocin is associated with positive emotions, such as happiness, contentment, and joy.

- It contributes to feelings of emotional warmth and well-being, promoting an overall positive mood.

- The emotional closeness experienced during social bonding releases oxytocin, contributing to feelings of happiness and satisfaction.

5. Parent-Child Bonding:

- Oxytocin plays a critical role in parent-child bonding, facilitating a strong emotional connection between parents and their children.

- It promotes nurturing behaviors and helps create a secure and loving environment for children.

6. Romantic Relationships:

- Oxytocin plays a significant role in romantic relationships, contributing to feelings of trust, intimacy, and attachment between partners.

- It is released during intimate moments, such as physical touch, cuddling, and sexual activity, strengthening the bond between romantic partners.

7. Social Reward and Reinforcement:

- Oxytocin reinforces positive social behaviors, making individuals more inclined to engage in pro-social actions, such as acts of kindness and cooperation.

- The positive feedback loop created by oxytocin release during social interactions reinforces the desire for further social bonding and connection.

B. Building Meaningful Relationships.

Building meaningful relationships involves establishing deep and authentic connections with others based on trust, mutual respect, and emotional intimacy. Meaningful relationships go beyond surface-level interactions and involve a genuine understanding and appreciation of each other's values, emotions, and experiences. These relationships provide a sense of belonging, support, and emotional fulfillment, contributing to overall well-being and life satisfaction. Here's a detailed explanation of how to build meaningful relationships:

1. Authenticity and Vulnerability:

- Be genuine and authentic in your interactions with others. Share your thoughts, feelings, and experiences openly and honestly.

- Embrace vulnerability by allowing yourself to be emotionally open and receptive to others' emotions and experiences.

2. Active Listening:

- Practice ***active and empathetic listening*** when engaging with others. Pay attention to their words, emotions, and non-verbal cues.

- Show genuine interest in their stories, concerns, and achievements.

3. Mutual Respect and Support:

- ***Treat others with respect and kindness***. Value their opinions and choices, even if they differ from your own.

- Be supportive and encouraging, especially during challenging times. Offer a helping hand and be a source of comfort and understanding.

4. Shared Values and Interests:

- Seek out individuals who share similar values, beliefs, and interests. Common ground forms a strong foundation for meaningful connections.

- Engage in activities and hobbies together to foster shared experiences and deepen the bond.

5. Emotional Intimacy:

- Share deeper emotions and feelings with trusted individuals. Emotional intimacy builds a stronger connection between people.

- Be receptive to the emotions and vulnerabilities shared by others and respond with empathy and compassion.

6. Effective Communication:

- Communicate clearly and openly, expressing your thoughts and feelings in a respectful manner.

- Be mindful of both verbal and non-verbal communication to ensure your message is conveyed effectively.

7. Trustworthiness:

- Be reliable and keep your promises. Building trust is essential for meaningful relationships.

- Trust is earned over time through consistent actions and genuine care for others.

8. Conflict Resolution:

- Handle conflicts with sensitivity and a willingness to understand the other person's perspective.

- Engage in constructive dialogue to find resolutions that benefit both parties and strengthen the relationship.

9. Empathy and Understanding:

- Practice empathy by putting yourself in the other person's shoes and trying to understand their feelings and experiences.

- Respect individual differences and perspectives, and avoid judgment.

10. Quality Time:

- Invest time and effort in nurturing your relationships. Spend quality time together, whether it's through one-on-one conversations or group activities.

- Prioritize your relationships and show that you value the people in your life.

Building meaningful relationships takes time and effort, but the rewards are well worth it. Meaningful connections provide a support system, a sense of belonging, and emotional fulfillment. They contribute to improved mental and emotional well-being and foster a positive and enriching social life. Remember that building meaningful relationships is a reciprocal process, and it requires effort from both parties to cultivate and sustain a deep and meaningful bond.

C. Acts of Kindness and Empathy.

Acts of kindness and empathy are powerful ways to connect with others and contribute positively to their well-being. Both kindness and empathy involve understanding and caring for the emotions and experiences of others, fostering a sense of compassion and support in various social interactions. Here's a detailed explanation of acts of kindness and empathy and their significance:

Acts of Kindness:

1. **Definition:** Acts of kindness refer to intentional gestures or actions that are done to benefit others without expecting anything in return. These acts can be big or small and may include helping, supporting, or showing compassion towards others.

2. **Impact:** Kindness has a profound impact on both the giver and the receiver. Performing acts of kindness can evoke positive emotions, such as happiness and satisfaction, in the person performing the act.

3. **Social Connection:** Acts of kindness foster social connections by creating a sense of shared humanity and goodwill. Kindness promotes a positive social environment and strengthens relationships.

4. **Stress Reduction:** Engaging in acts of kindness can reduce stress and anxiety for both the giver and the receiver. Kindness triggers the release of **oxytocin, the "love hormone,"** which promotes feelings of calm and well-being.

5. **Modeling Behavior:** Acts of kindness can inspire others to engage in similar behaviors, creating a

ripple effect of positivity and compassion in the community.

6. **Boosting Mental Health:** Regularly practicing kindness is associated with improved mental health, increased life satisfaction, and reduced feelings of loneliness.

Empathy:

1. **Definition:** Empathy is the ability to understand and share the feelings and perspectives of others. It involves putting yourself in someone else's shoes and experiencing their emotions from their point of view.

2. **Active Listening:** Empathy is facilitated through active listening, where you pay close attention to the person's words, emotions, and body language.

3. **Validation and Understanding:** Demonstrating empathy involves acknowledging the other person's feelings and validating their experiences. It helps individuals feel heard and supported.

4. **Strengthening Relationships:** Empathy is a key component of building meaningful relationships. It fosters trust, emotional intimacy, and a deeper sense of connection between individuals.

5. **Conflict Resolution:** Empathy is essential in resolving conflicts and misunderstandings. It allows for better communication and a willingness to find solutions that meet both parties' needs.

6. **Cultivating Compassion:** Empathy nurtures compassion and fosters a caring attitude towards

others. It encourages acts of kindness and supportive behavior.

Combining Kindness and Empathy:

1. **Deepening Connection:** When acts of kindness are paired with empathy, they become more meaningful and impactful. Understanding the emotions and needs of others enables us to offer the right type of support and care.

2. **Support during Challenges:** Combining kindness and empathy helps individuals provide genuine support and comfort during difficult times. It strengthens emotional bonds and creates a safe space for vulnerability.

3. **Reducing Stigma:** Empathetic acts of kindness combat stigma and discrimination by showing understanding and acceptance towards those facing challenges or adversity.

4. **Promoting Inclusivity:** Acts of kindness and empathy promote inclusivity and respect for diverse perspectives and experiences.

5. **Positive Influence:** Demonstrating kindness and empathy can inspire others to be more compassionate and considerate in their interactions.

Practicing acts of kindness and empathy enhances our social connections and contributes to a more compassionate and supportive community. It strengthens relationships, boosts emotional well-being, and fosters a positive social environment. By cultivating these qualities in our interactions with others, we can create a more empathetic and kinder world.

QUIZ TIME

1. What is the significance of social connections in an individual's life?

A) Social connections have no impact on well-being.

B) Social connections solely lead to stress and emotional burden.

C) Positive social connections contribute to increased happiness, emotional support, and a sense of belonging.

D) Social connections solely affect physical health, not emotional experiences.

2. How can strong relationships positively impact an individual's well-being?

A) Strong relationships have no impact on well-being.

B) Strong relationships lead to isolation and decreased happiness.

C) Strong relationships provide emotional support, reduce stress, and enhance overall happiness.

D) Strong relationships solely affect external behaviors, not emotional experiences.

3. What is the connection between oxytocin and social bonding?

A) Oxytocin is unrelated to social bonding or happiness.

B) Oxytocin is only relevant to physical health.

C) Oxytocin is a neurotransmitter that plays a key role in fostering social bonds and feelings of connection.

D) Oxytocin solely affects external behaviors, not internal processes.

4. How does volunteering or acts of service contribute to happiness?

A) Volunteering has no impact on happiness.

B) Volunteering solely benefits the external community, not personal well-being.

C) Acts of service lead to decreased happiness and emotional burden.

D) Volunteering fosters a sense of purpose, connection, and fulfillment, contributing to happiness.

5. How can individuals practice empathy to enhance their relationships?

A) Empathy has no impact on relationships or happiness.

B) By avoiding emotional connections with others.

C) By actively listening, understanding others' perspectives, and showing genuine care and compassion.

D) Empathy solely affects physical health, not emotional experiences.

Answers: 1. (C) 2. (C) 3. (C) 4. (D) 5. (C)

****

Chapter 8: Tapping into Endorphins for Pain Relief and Euphoria

"The greatest discovery of all time is that a person can change their future by merely changing their attitude." - Oprah Winfrey

****

Oil of Wisdom: Navigating Life's Marvels and Morals

Once upon a time, there was a father who wanted his son to learn the secret of happiness from the wisest man in the world. The father sent his son on a journey to find this wise man. The boy's journey led him through a desert, and after forty days, he arrived at a beautiful castle atop a mountain. This castle was where the wisest man lived.

However, when the boy entered the castle, he found it bustling with activity. There were tradesmen coming and going, people chatting everywhere, and even a small orchestra playing music. The main room was filled with delicious food from all over the world. It seemed more like a busy marketplace than the serene dwelling of a wise man.

Finally, after waiting for two hours, the boy got a chance to speak with the wise man. He explained why he had come and asked for the secret of happiness. The wise man listened, but he told the boy that he couldn't explain the secret right then. Instead, he suggested the boy explore the palace for two hours and then return.

Before the boy left, the wise man gave him a teaspoon with two drops of oil and asked him to carry it without spilling. The boy walked around the palace, carefully holding the spoon and focusing on not spilling the oil. After two hours, he returned to the wise man.

The wise man asked if the boy had observed the marvels of his castle, like the tapestries, the gardens, and the library. Embarrassed, the boy admitted he hadn't noticed anything because he was focused on the spoon and the oil. The wise man told him to go back and observe everything while keeping the drops of oil safe.

The boy followed the wise man's advice and began to truly see the beauty around him. He noticed the art, the gardens, and the scenery. When he returned to the wise man and recounted what he had seen, the wise man asked about the drops of oil. The boy realized they were gone, and he felt worried.

The wise man then shared his advice: ***The secret of happiness is to appreciate the marvels of the world around you but never forget who you are and the values you hold.*** Just like the drops of oil on the spoon, even as you explore the world and enjoy its wonders, remember your identity and your ethics. The boy learned that ***true happiness comes from a balance of experiencing the world while staying true to oneself.***

≈ ≈ ≈

Endorphins are natural chemicals produced by the body that act as neurotransmitters in the brain. They are often referred to as **"feel-good" chemicals** because they play a key role in relieving pain and promoting feelings of euphoria and well-being. Endorphins are released in response to certain stimuli, including physical exercise, stress, pain, and pleasurable activities. Here's a detailed explanation of how endorphins work and their significance in pain relief and promoting euphoria:

A. Understanding Endorphins' Role in Happiness and Pain Management.

Endorphins play a significant role in both happiness and pain management. These naturally occurring chemicals, known as neurotransmitters, are produced by the body and act as messengers in the brain. They are primarily associated with the body's response to stress, pain, and pleasure. Here's a detailed explanation of how endorphins influence happiness and pain management:

1. Role in Happiness:

- **Euphoria and Positive Emotions:** Endorphins are often referred to as **"feel-good"** chemicals because they can induce feelings of euphoria and well-being. When endorphins are released, they interact with the brain's opioid receptors, triggering positive emotional responses.

- **Hedonic Reward System:** Endorphins are part of the brain's hedonic reward system, which reinforces behaviors that are essential for survival and pleasure. Engaging in activities that stimulate endorphin release, such as exercise, laughter, or enjoyable experiences, leads to a sense of reward and motivates individuals to repeat these behaviors.

- **Stress Reduction:** Endorphins act as natural stress reducers. They counteract the effects of stress hormones, such as **cortisol,** by promoting relaxation and reducing anxiety. Engaging in activities that trigger endorphin release can help alleviate feelings of stress and promote a sense of calm.

- **Exercise and Endorphins:** Physical exercise, particularly aerobic activities like running, swimming, or dancing, is a potent trigger for endorphin release. This is commonly referred to as the **"runner's high."** The increase in endorphins during exercise contributes to the feelings of pleasure and satisfaction often experienced after a workout.

- **Social Bonding:** Endorphin release during certain activities, like group exercises or bonding experiences, can promote social bonding and a sense of connection with others. Participating in shared activities that lead to endorphin release can strengthen social connections.

2. Role in Pain Management:

- **Natural Painkillers:** Endorphins act as natural painkillers in the body. When the body experiences pain, endorphins are released and bind to opioid receptors in the brain and spinal cord. This interaction blocks the transmission of pain signals and reduces the perception of pain.

- **Coping Mechanism for Pain:** Engaging in activities that trigger endorphin release can help individuals cope with pain and discomfort. This is why activities like exercise, which stimulate endorphin release, can be beneficial for individuals dealing with chronic pain or recovering from injuries.

- **Pain Modulation:** Endorphins play a role in modulating pain perception. They can affect the brain's interpretation of pain signals, leading to a decreased perception of pain intensity.

- **Postoperative and Natural Pain Relief:** Endorphins are involved in the body's response to pain following surgeries and injuries. Additionally, the body releases endorphins during childbirth, which contributes to the natural pain relief experienced by some women during labor.

Understanding the role of endorphins in happiness and pain management highlights their importance in promoting overall well-being. Engaging in activities that trigger endorphin release, such as exercise, laughter, or spending time with loved ones, can enhance mood, reduce stress, and alleviate pain. Additionally, incorporating such activities into daily life can lead to a more positive outlook, improved emotional resilience, and a heightened sense of happiness and fulfillment.

B. The Power of Physical Activity and Exercise.

Physical activity and exercise have a profound impact on overall health and well-being. They offer a wide range of physical, mental, and emotional benefits that contribute to a healthier and happier life. Here's a detailed explanation of the power of physical activity and exercise:

1. Physical Health Benefits:

- **Weight Management:** Regular exercise helps with weight management by burning calories and increasing metabolism.

- **Cardiovascular Health:** Exercise improves heart health by strengthening the heart muscle, lowering blood pressure, and increasing **HDL (good) cholesterol levels.**

- **Bone Health:** Weight-bearing exercises, such as walking or weightlifting, promote bone density and reduce the risk of osteoporosis.

- **Muscle Strength and Flexibility:** Exercise builds and tones muscles, enhancing overall strength and flexibility.

- **Improved Immune System:** Regular physical activity can boost the immune system, making the body more resilient to infections and illnesses.

2. Mental Health Benefits:

- **Stress Reduction:** Exercise triggers the release of **endorphins**, which are natural stress-relieving hormones, leading to reduced feelings of stress and anxiety.

- **Mood Enhancement:** Physical activity stimulates the production of neurotransmitters, such as **serotonin and dopamine**, which are associated with feelings of happiness and pleasure.

- **Improved Cognitive Function:** Regular exercise has been linked to enhanced cognitive function, improved memory, and increased focus.

- **Better Sleep:** Physical activity can promote better sleep quality and help with insomnia or sleep disturbances.

- **Reduced Risk of Depression:** Exercise has antidepressant effects and can reduce the risk of developing depression.

3. Increased Energy and Endurance:

- **Boosted Energy Levels:** Regular physical activity leads to increased energy levels and reduced feelings of fatigue.

- **Improved Endurance:** Exercise improves cardiovascular fitness, allowing individuals to engage in daily activities with greater ease.

4. Disease Prevention:

- **Type 2 Diabetes:** Regular exercise can help prevent and manage type 2 diabetes by improving insulin sensitivity and blood sugar control.

- **Cancer Risk Reduction:** Physical activity has been associated with a reduced risk of certain types of cancer, such as breast and colon cancer.

- **Chronic Diseases:** Exercise can help manage and reduce the risk of chronic conditions, such as hypertension and metabolic syndrome.

5. Social Benefits:

- **Opportunities for Social Interaction:** Group exercises, sports, and fitness classes provide opportunities to meet and socialize with like-minded individuals.

- **Enhanced Social Support:** Engaging in physical activities with others fosters a sense of camaraderie and social support.

6. Longevity:

- **Increased Lifespan:** Regular exercise has been linked to increased life expectancy and a reduced risk of premature mortality.

7. Enhanced Self-Confidence and Body Image:

- **Improved Body Image:** Engaging in regular exercise can improve body image and self-esteem.

- **Sense of Achievement:** Setting and achieving exercise goals can boost self-confidence and self-efficacy.

8. Adaptable and Accessible:

- **Varied Options:** There are numerous forms of physical activity and exercise to suit individual preferences, including walking, cycling, swimming, dancing, yoga, strength training, and more.

- **Accessibility:** Exercise can be done almost anywhere, whether at home, in a gym, outdoors, or in group settings.

9. Brain Health:

- **Neuroplasticity:** Exercise supports neuroplasticity, the brain's ability to adapt and reorganize neural connections, which is crucial for learning and memory.

- **Reduced Cognitive Decline:** Regular exercise has been associated with a reduced risk of cognitive decline and neurodegenerative diseases, such as Alzheimer's.

10. Emotional Well-being:

- **Emotional Release:** Exercise can serve as a healthy outlet for pent-up emotions and stress.

- **Improved Coping Skills:** Regular physical activity can enhance coping skills, leading to better resilience in the face of challenges.

Incorporating regular physical activity and exercise into one's lifestyle can lead to significant improvements in physical and mental health. The combination of physical benefits, such as weight management and improved cardiovascular health, along with the positive impact on mood, stress reduction, and enhanced cognitive function, makes exercise a powerful tool for promoting overall well-being. Whether it's a structured exercise routine or simply staying active through daily activities, the benefits of physical activity are vast and can contribute to a happier, healthier, and more fulfilling life.

C. Laughter and Other Activities that Trigger Endorphin Release.

Activities that trigger endorphin release have the power to improve mood, reduce stress, and enhance overall well-being. Laughter, in particular, is one of the most effective ways to stimulate endorphin production. Additionally, engaging in various other activities can also lead to the release of these **"feel-good" chemicals**. Here's a detailed explanation of laughter and other activities that trigger endorphin release:

1. Laughter:

- **Endorphin Release:** Laughter triggers the release of endorphins in the brain. When we laugh, the **brain's opioid receptors** are activated, leading to feelings of pleasure and euphoria.

- **Stress Reduction:** Laughter has a powerful stress-reducing effect. It lowers cortisol levels, the hormone associated with stress, and promotes relaxation.

- **Improved Mood:** Laughing can enhance mood and provide a sense of joy and happiness.

- **Social Bonding:** Laughter is often a social activity, and sharing laughter with others fosters social bonding and strengthens relationships.

- **Immune System Boost:** The positive effects of laughter on the immune system have been studied. Regular laughter has been shown to boost immune function.

2. Exercise:

- **Endorphin Release:** As mentioned earlier, physical exercise triggers the release of endorphins. Activities like running, cycling, dancing, or any form of aerobic exercise can lead to the ***"runner's high,"*** characterized by feelings of euphoria and well-being.

- **Stress Reduction:** Regular exercise is a potent stress reliever. It helps reduce cortisol levels and promotes relaxation.

- **Improved Sleep:** Engaging in regular exercise can lead to better sleep quality, contributing to overall well-being.

- **Enhanced Self-Confidence:** Achieving exercise goals and experiencing the benefits of improved physical fitness can boost self-confidence.

3. Listening to Music:

- **Endorphin Release:** Listening to music that evokes positive emotions can trigger the release of endorphins in the brain.

- **Mood Enhancement:** Music can have a profound impact on mood, helping to reduce stress and anxiety.

- **Emotional Release:** Music can serve as an emotional outlet, allowing individuals to express and process their emotions.

4. Engaging in Creative Activities:

- **Endorphin Release:** Engaging in creative activities like painting, writing, or crafting can stimulate endorphin release.

- **Positive Emotional Experience:** Creative expression can lead to a sense of accomplishment and emotional fulfillment.

5. Acts of Kindness:

- **Endorphin Release:** Performing acts of kindness and helping others can trigger the release of endorphins.

- **Emotional Reward:** Acts of kindness generate positive emotions, contributing to a sense of happiness and well-being.

6. Physical Affection:

- **Endorphin Release:** Physical affection, such as hugging or cuddling, can stimulate endorphin production.

- **Enhanced Social Connection:** Physical affection fosters a sense of connection and intimacy in relationships.

7. Meditation and Mindfulness:

- **Endorphin Release:** Engaging in mindfulness practices and meditation can lead to the release of endorphins.

- **Stress Reduction:** Meditation and mindfulness help reduce stress and promote a sense of calm.

8. Spending Time in Nature:

- **Endorphin Release:** Being in nature and experiencing the beauty of the outdoors can trigger endorphin release.

- **Improved Mood:** Nature exposure is associated with enhanced mood and reduced feelings of stress.

9. Socializing and Spending Time with Loved Ones:

- **Endorphin Release:** Social interactions and spending time with loved ones can lead to endorphin release.

- **Social Bonding:** Positive social interactions strengthen relationships and contribute to overall happiness.

10. Sunlight Exposure:

- **Endorphin Release:** Sunlight exposure can lead to the release of endorphins and a boost in mood.

- **Vitamin D Production:** Sunlight exposure is essential for the body's production of vitamin D, which plays a role in overall health.

Engaging in activities that trigger endorphin release is a powerful way to improve mood, reduce stress, and promote overall well-being. From laughter and exercise to creative expression and acts of kindness, these activities contribute to a positive and fulfilling life. Incorporating such activities into daily life can lead to a happier and more balanced existence, fostering emotional resilience and enhancing overall quality of life.

<h1 style="text-align:center">QUIZ TIME</h1>

1. What is the primary focus of, "Tapping into Endorphins for Pain Relief and Euphoria"?

A) Analyzing the role of brain chemistry in social interactions.

B) Exploring the impact of external factors on happiness.

C) Understanding the influence of endorphins on pain and joy.

D) Examining the connection between habits and physical health.

2. What is the role of endorphins in the body?

A) Endorphins have no impact on the body's functioning.

B) Endorphins are solely related to physical pain management.

C) Endorphins are neurotransmitters that contribute to pain relief and positive emotions.

D) Endorphins only affect external behaviors, not internal processes.

3. How do endorphins contribute to feelings of euphoria?

A) Endorphins have no impact on euphoria.

B) Endorphins solely lead to increased stress and anxiety.

C) Endorphins interact with the brain's receptors to create a sense of pleasure and well-being.

D) Euphoria is solely determined by external circumstances.

4. What is the relationship between endorphins and physical activity?

A) Physical activity has no impact on endorphin release.

B) Endorphin release is solely triggered by external factors.

C) Physical activity stimulates the release of endorphins, contributing to pain relief and happiness. D) Endorphin release only affects emotional experiences, not physical health.

5. How does laughter contribute to the release of endorphins?

A) Laughter has no impact on endorphin release.

B) Laughter solely leads to increased stress and emotional burden.

C) Laughter triggers the release of endorphins, promoting a sense of joy and well-being.

D) Endorphin release solely affects physical health, not emotional experiences.

Answers: 1. (C) 2. (C) 3. (C) 4. (C) 5. (C)

****

Chapter 9: Creating Sustainable Joy

"Happiness is not something you postpone for the future; it is something you design for the present." - Jim Rohn

****

The Mirror Effect: What You Give, You Get

Once upon a time, there was a person who moved to a new village. He was curious about whether he would like his new home. He decided to seek advice from a wise Zen master in the village.

He approached the Zen master and asked, "Do you think I will like this village? Are the people nice?"

The master replied with a question, "How were the people in the town you came from?"

The newcomer sighed and said, "They were nasty and greedy. They were always angry and engaged in dishonesty and stealing."

The master calmly nodded and said, "Well, those are exactly the type of people we have in this village."

A day later, another newcomer arrived in the village and went to visit the Zen master with the same question. He asked, "Will I like this village? Are the people here kind?"

The master, as before, asked, "How were the people in the town you come from?"

The newcomer smiled and answered, "They were sweet and lived in harmony. They cared for each other. They respected one another and were spiritual seekers."

The master nodded again and said, "Well, those are exactly the type of people we have in this village."

You see, in life, whatever you perceive in the world, the world will perceive in you. If you see hope, goodness, and love, the world will see the same in you. But if you only see the negative aspects of people, that's what they will see in you.

So, it's important to be good to the world, and the world will be good to you. If you give love to the world, the world will give love to you in return. Remember, *your perspective shapes your reality.*

And so, the lesson from the village is simple: *See the best in others, spread kindness, and positivity will reflect back onto you.*

≈ ≈ ≈

Creating sustainable joy involves adopting practices and making lifestyle choices that promote long-lasting happiness and well-being. It goes beyond momentary pleasures and aims to cultivate a positive and fulfilling life that endures through both the ups and downs. Here's a detailed explanation of how to create sustainable joy:

1. Cultivating Positive Mindset:

- **Focus on gratitude:** Regularly express gratitude for the positive aspects of life. Gratitude shifts the focus towards the good, leading to increased happiness.

- **Practice positive affirmations:** Use positive affirmations to foster a constructive and optimistic mindset.

- **Reframe negative thoughts:** When faced with challenges, try to reframe negative thoughts into more positive and empowering ones.

2. Pursuing Meaning and Purpose:

- **Identify passions and interests:** Discover activities and pursuits that bring a sense of fulfillment and align with personal values.

- **Set meaningful goals:** Set clear and achievable goals that contribute to personal growth and align with broader life values.

- **Engage in acts of service:** Helping others and contributing to the community can provide a sense of purpose and fulfillment.

3. Nurturing Relationships:

- **Prioritize quality time:** Dedicate time to nurture meaningful relationships with family and friends.

- **Communicate openly:** Maintain honest and open communication in relationships to foster trust and emotional intimacy.

- **Be supportive and empathetic:** Show care and understanding towards others' emotions and experiences.

4. Practicing Self-Compassion:

- **Treat yourself kindly:** Avoid self-criticism and practice self-compassion during challenging times.

- **Prioritize self-care:** Make time for activities that promote physical, mental, and emotional well-being.

- **Embrace imperfections:** Accept that nobody is perfect, and mistakes are a natural part of life.

5. Embracing Resilience:

- **Develop coping skills:** Cultivate coping strategies to handle stress and adversity effectively.

- **View challenges as opportunities:** Reframe challenges as learning experiences that promote personal growth.

- **Seek support when needed:** Reach out to friends, family, or professionals for support during difficult times.

6. Balancing Work and Leisure:

- **Set boundaries:** Establish a healthy work-life balance to prevent burnout and maintain overall well-being.

- **Engage in leisure activities:** Participate in hobbies and activities that bring joy and relaxation.

7. Being Mindful and Present:

- **Practice mindfulness:** Be present in the moment and engage fully in daily activities.

- **Savor positive experiences:** Appreciate and savor the joyful moments in life.

8. Gratitude and Acts of Kindness:

- **Express gratitude:** Regularly acknowledge and express gratitude for the positive aspects of life.

- **Perform acts of kindness:** Engage in acts of kindness towards others, which can promote happiness and foster social connections.

9. Continual Growth and Learning:

- **Embrace a growth mindset:** View challenges and failures as opportunities for growth and learning.

- **Pursue learning opportunities:** Engage in activities that expand knowledge and skills.

10. Connection with Nature:

- **Spend time outdoors:** Connect with nature regularly to reduce stress and enhance well-being.

- **Practice eco-friendly habits:** Engaging in sustainable practices can promote a sense of connection to the environment.

Creating sustainable joy is an ongoing process that involves making conscious choices and cultivating positive habits. By focusing on gratitude, meaningful pursuits, nurturing relationships, and self-compassion, you can create a fulfilling and happy life that endures through various life circumstances. Sustainable joy is not about constant euphoria but rather about a deep sense of contentment and well-being that remains present amidst life's challenges and joys. By incorporating these practices into your daily life, you can foster lasting happiness and lead a more fulfilling and meaningful existence.

A. The Importance of Balance and Self-Care.

The importance of balance and self-care cannot be overstated when it comes to maintaining overall well-being and sustainable happiness. These two elements are essential for leading a fulfilling life and managing the various demands and challenges that arise. Here's a detailed elaboration on the significance of balance and self-care:

1. Balance:

- **Physical Health:** Striking a balance in physical health involves maintaining a healthy lifestyle that includes regular exercise, proper nutrition, and sufficient rest. It also means avoiding extremes and finding a middle ground in activities to prevent burnout or excessive strain on the body.

- **Mental Health:** Balance in mental health involves managing stress levels, practicing mindfulness, and cultivating a positive mindset. It also means recognizing the need for breaks and relaxation to avoid mental exhaustion.

- **Work-Life Balance:** Balancing work and personal life is crucial for preventing work-related stress and maintaining healthy relationships. Allowing time for personal interests, hobbies, and spending quality time with loved ones is essential for overall well-being.

- **Emotional Balance:** Acknowledging and processing emotions in a healthy way is vital for emotional balance. Avoiding emotional suppression and finding healthy outlets for expressing emotions fosters emotional resilience.

- **Social Life:** Striking a balance in social interactions means nurturing meaningful relationships without neglecting personal boundaries or feeling overwhelmed by social obligations.

2. Self-Care:

- **Physical Self-Care:** Taking care of one's physical well-being through regular exercise, proper nutrition, adequate sleep, and medical check-ups.

- **Emotional Self-Care:** Practicing self-compassion, acknowledging emotions, and engaging in activities that promote emotional well-being, such as journaling or talking to a supportive friend.

- **Mental Self-Care:** Engaging in activities that stimulate the mind, such as reading, learning new skills, or engaging in creative pursuits.

- **Social Self-Care:** Prioritizing meaningful connections and nurturing relationships with friends and family.

- **Spiritual Self-Care:** Engaging in activities that foster a sense of purpose and connection, such as meditation, spending time in nature, or volunteering.

- **Setting Boundaries:** Practicing self-care involves setting healthy boundaries with others to protect one's well-being and prevent emotional burnout.

3. Benefits of Balance and Self-Care:

- **Reduced Stress:** Finding balance in life and practicing self-care can significantly reduce stress levels, promoting better physical and mental health.

- **Enhanced Resilience:** Balancing various aspects of life and caring for oneself fosters emotional resilience, helping individuals cope with challenges more effectively.

- **Improved Physical Health:** Engaging in self-care practices and maintaining balance in daily activities contribute to better physical health and overall vitality.

- **Mental Clarity and Focus:** Self-care practices and life balance can lead to improved focus and mental clarity, enhancing productivity and decision-making.

- **Emotional Well-Being:** Prioritizing self-care and finding balance can lead to greater emotional well-being and a more positive outlook on life.

- **Healthy Relationships:** Balancing personal and social life and practicing self-care can lead to healthier and more fulfilling relationships with others.

4. Avoiding Burnout:

- Practicing balance and self-care is essential for preventing burnout, which occurs when you become emotionally, mentally, and physically exhausted due to prolonged stress and excessive demands.

- Burnout can negatively impact overall health, work performance, and personal relationships.

- Prioritizing self-care and maintaining a balanced life helps you avoid burnout and promotes a healthier, happier, and more sustainable lifestyle.

We must remember that balance and self-care are foundational aspects of leading a fulfilling and sustainable life. By recognizing the importance of finding equilibrium in various areas of life and making time for self-care practices, you can enhance your physical and mental well-being, reduce stress, and foster healthy relationships. Striving for balance and self-care is a continuous journey that contributes to a happier, healthier, and more resilient life.

B. Combining Strategies for Optimal Happiness.

Combining strategies for optimal happiness involves integrating various evidence-based approaches and practices to create a comprehensive and holistic approach to well-being. By combining different strategies, you can amplify your positive impact, address multiple aspects of life, and cultivate sustainable joy. Here's an explanation of how to combine strategies for optimal happiness:

1. Mind-Body Connection:

- Recognize the interplay between physical and mental well-being. Engage in regular exercise to trigger endorphin release and reduce stress, which can positively impact mood and emotional well-being.

- Practice mindfulness and meditation to cultivate a positive mindset, reduce anxiety, and enhance self-awareness.

2. Building Positive Relationships:

- Cultivate meaningful social connections with family, friends, and community members. Spending time with loved ones and engaging in acts of kindness can trigger the release of endorphins and promote feelings of happiness.

- Encourage laughter and fun in social interactions to create a positive and joyful atmosphere.

3. Pursuing Passion and Purpose:

- Identify passions and interests that bring a sense of fulfillment. Setting and achieving meaningful goals can lead to a sense of purpose and accomplishment.

- Engage in acts of service and contribute to causes that align with personal values, fostering a deeper sense of purpose and happiness.

4. Self-Compassion and Self-Care:

- Practice self-compassion by treating oneself with kindness and understanding during challenging times.

- Prioritize self-care by engaging in activities that promote physical, emotional, and mental well-being. This can include exercise, hobbies, journaling, and spending time in nature.

5. Gratitude and Positivity:

- Cultivate a habit of gratitude by regularly acknowledging and appreciating the positive aspects of life.

- Practice positive thinking and affirmations to promote a constructive mindset.

6. Balancing Work and Leisure:

- Establish a healthy work-life balance to prevent burnout and ensure sufficient time for personal activities and relaxation.

- Engage in leisure activities that bring joy and help recharge the mind and body.

7. Mindful Consumption:

- Be mindful of media consumption and its impact on mental well-being. Limit exposure to negative or stressful content and focus on uplifting and inspiring material.

8. Nature and Environment:

- Spend time in nature to trigger endorphin release and reduce stress.

- Create a positive and pleasant living and working environment that promotes well-being.

9. Continuous Growth and Learning:

- Embrace a growth mindset and view challenges as opportunities for learning and personal development.

- Engage in continuous learning to stimulate the mind and foster a sense of achievement.

10. Acts of Kindness and Giving Back:

- Engage in acts of kindness and giving back to others, as these actions not only benefit others but also trigger the release of endorphins and promote feelings of happiness.

Combining these strategies creates a synergistic effect, enhancing overall well-being and contributing to sustainable joy. By adopting a multifaceted approach that addresses physical, emotional, social, and spiritual aspects of life, you can optimize your happiness and lead a more fulfilling and meaningful existence. Customizing these strategies to suit individual preferences and needs ensures that the pursuit of optimal happiness aligns with personal values and goals. Ultimately, the combination of these evidence-based approaches empowers you to create a balanced and joyful life that endures through various life circumstances.

C. Overcoming Challenges and Setbacks.

Overcoming challenges and setbacks is an essential aspect of life that allows you to grow, develop resilience, and continue moving forward. Life is filled with ups and downs, and facing obstacles is a natural part of the human experience. Here's an explanation of how to overcome challenges and setbacks effectively:

1. Acceptance and Acknowledgment:

- Acknowledge the reality of the situation and accept that setbacks are a normal part of life.

- Allow yourself to feel and process emotions related to the challenge without judgment.

2. Positive Mindset and Self-Compassion:

- Cultivate a positive mindset and focus on potential solutions rather than dwelling on the problem.

- Practice self-compassion and avoid self-blame. Be kind to yourself during difficult times.

3. Seek Support:

- Reach out to friends, family, or support networks for emotional and practical assistance.

- Talking to others about the challenges can provide fresh perspectives and insights.

4. Problem-Solving and Planning:

- Analyze the situation and break the challenge into manageable steps.

- Create a plan to address the issue and take action on each step.

5. Adaptability and Flexibility:

- Be open to adjusting plans and strategies if needed. Sometimes, the initial approach may need modification as new information or obstacles arise.

- Embrace adaptability and flexibility to navigate unexpected changes.

6. Learning Opportunities:

- View challenges and setbacks as opportunities for growth and learning.

- Identify lessons that can be learned from the experience and use them to improve future decision-making and problem-solving.

7. Resilience and Perseverance:

- Cultivate resilience, which is the ability to bounce back and recover from adversity.

- Persevere through difficult times and maintain focus on long-term goals.

8. Positive Coping Mechanisms:

- Engage in healthy and positive coping mechanisms, such as exercise, mindfulness, or spending time with loved ones.

- Avoid harmful coping strategies, such as excessive alcohol consumption or withdrawal from social interactions.

9. Break Tasks into Smaller Steps:

- If a challenge feels overwhelming, break it down into smaller, more achievable tasks.

- Focus on completing one step at a time, which can lead to a sense of progress and motivation.

10. Celebrate Progress:

- Acknowledge and celebrate even small successes along the way.

- Celebrating progress, no matter how minor, can boost motivation and build momentum.

11. Seek Professional Help if Needed:

- If a challenge seems insurmountable or is affecting mental or emotional well-being, consider seeking professional support, such as counseling or therapy.

12. Maintain Perspective:

- Keep the bigger picture in mind and avoid catastrophizing.

- Recognize that setbacks are temporary, and with time and effort, they can be overcome.

Overcoming challenges and setbacks requires resilience, determination, and a positive mindset. By approaching obstacles with a solution-oriented mindset and seeking support when needed, you can navigate through difficult times successfully. Challenges can serve as opportunities for personal growth and provide valuable life lessons, ultimately contributing to increased strength and wisdom. The journey of overcoming challenges is an integral part of self-discovery and empowerment, shaping you into more resilient and capable beings.

QUIZ TIME

1. What do we mean by, "Creating Sustainable Joy"?

A) Analyzing the impact of external factors on happiness.

B) Exploring the role of brain chemistry in sustaining joy.

C) Understanding the importance of cultivating lasting happiness.

D) Examining the connection between habits and physical health.

2. How do you define "sustainable joy"?

A) Sustainable joy is unattainable and solely exists in fairy tales.

 B) Sustainable joy is a temporary state unrelated to habits or mindset.

C) Sustainable joy refers to a deep sense of contentment and happiness that endures over time.

D) Sustainable joy is solely determined by external circumstances.

3. Why is balance essential for creating sustainable joy?

A) Balance has no impact on joy or well-being.

 B) Balance prevents any experience of joy.

C) Balance allows individuals to avoid challenges and setbacks.

D) Balance helps individuals manage stress, avoid burnout, and maintain long-term happiness.

4. How self-care contributes to sustainable joy?

A) Self-care has no impact on joy or well-being.

 B) Self-care solely involves physical activities.

C) Self-care promotes emotional well-being, reduces stress, and supports sustained happiness.

D) Self-care is solely related to external factors, not internal experiences.

5. How does the pursuit of passions and interests relate to creating sustainable joy?

A) Pursuit of passions and interests has no impact on joy.

B) Pursuit of passions and interests solely leads to stress and emotional burden.

 C) Engaging in activities that align with one's passions contributes to a sense of purpose and long-lasting happiness.

D) Pursuit of passions is solely determined by external factors.

Answers: 1. (C) 2. (C) 3 (D) 4. (C) 5. (C)

****

Chapter 10: Conclusion

"Life is 10% what happens to us and 90% how we react to it." - Charles R. Swindoll

****

In the journey of life, the pursuit of happiness is an endeavor that resonates with every human heart. **"The Happiness Amplifier"** has illuminated a path towards achieving not just fleeting moments of happiness, but a profound and enduring sense of well-being that accompanies us through every twist and turn.

Throughout this exploration, we've delved into the *seven secrets* that act as the keys to unlocking sustainable joy:

1. **Mindfulness and Present Living:**

    The power of now is undeniable. By grounding ourselves in the present moment, we free ourselves from the shackles of past regrets and future anxieties. Embracing mindfulness enables us to savor life's simplest pleasures and cultivate a profound appreciation for the beauty that surrounds us.

2. **Gratitude and Positive Perspective:**

    The act of gratitude is a beacon of light in our lives. Shifting our focus to what we have, rather than what we lack, infuses our days with positivity. As we acknowledge the blessings that often go unnoticed, we plant the seeds of happiness in the fertile soil of gratitude.

3. **Fostering Meaning and Purpose:**

In the tapestry of our existence, weaving threads of meaning and purpose adds vibrant hues. By identifying our passions, setting meaningful goals, and contributing to the greater good, we sculpt a life that resonates deeply with our soul's yearnings.

4. **Nurturing Authentic Relationships:**

The connections we forge with others are the pillars that uphold our joy. The warmth of genuine relationships, forged through open communication, empathy, and shared experiences, fuels our sense of belonging and enriches our lives immeasurably.

5. **Embracing Resilience:**

Life's challenges are the crucibles that shape our character. Embracing resilience transforms setbacks into stepping stones. By cultivating an unwavering spirit, we develop the strength to weather storms and emerge stronger, wiser, and more compassionate.

6. **Practicing Self-Compassion:**

In the mirror of self-compassion, we glimpse our true essence. Treating ourselves with kindness during difficult times and nurturing our well-being through *self-care* is an act of *self-love* that radiates outward, uplifting not only ourselves but those around us.

7. **Amplifying Joy through Endorphins:**
The body and mind are inextricably linked, and harnessing the natural power of endorphins deepens our experience of joy. Whether through laughter, physical activity, or acts of kindness, triggering the release of these **"feel-good"** chemicals is a gateway to sustainable happiness.

By integrating these *seven secrets* into our lives, we have the potential to elevate our well-being to new heights. Sustainable joy is not a fleeting dream but a reality within our grasp. It's a state of being that endures, not only through calm seas but also through the tempests that life inevitably brings.

As we close the pages of **"The Happiness Amplifier,"** let us embark on a new chapter with a renewed perspective. Let us commit to the daily practice of joy cultivation, infusing our lives with **mindfulness, gratitude, purpose, authentic connections, resilience, self-compassion, and endorphin-fueled elation**.

May your life be a testament to the boundless potential of happiness amplification? May you be a beacon of joy, inspiring others to unlock the secrets of a blissful life. And may your days be illuminated by the radiant light of sustainable joy, guiding you towards a life well-lived and deeply cherished.

****

BOOK SUMMARY

Chapter 1: Understanding Happiness

- Happiness is a complex emotional state encompassing positive emotions, life satisfaction, and a sense of well-being.

- Factors influencing happiness include genetics, life circumstances, and intentional activities.

- Subjective well-being measures include life evaluation, positive emotions, and negative emotions.

- The **"hedonic treadmill"** concept explains how we adapt to positive or negative changes, returning to a baseline level of happiness.

- Happiness is influenced by internal factors **(mindset, genetics)** and external factors **(relationships, environment).**

Chapter 2: Understanding Happiness

- Happiness is linked to a strengthened immune system, improved cardiovascular health, and effective pain management.

- Positive emotions trigger the release of endorphins, which reduce stress and enhance pain tolerance.

- Meaningful relationships contribute to a sense of belonging, trust, and overall life satisfaction.

- The hedonic treadmill refers to the tendency of happiness levels to return to a baseline despite positive or negative events.

- Cultivating gratitude to appreciate existing positive aspects of life.

Chapter 3: The Interplay of Brain Chemistry and Habits

- Brain chemistry, governed by neurotransmitters like **serotonin and dopamine**, impacts emotions and mood.

- Habits are ingrained behavioral patterns that affect brain function and neurotransmitter release.

- **Neuroplasticity** is the brain's ability to adapt and reorganize in response to learning and experiences.

- Experience-dependent, developmental, and adaptive plasticity are types of neuroplasticity.

- Positive habits and understanding neuroplasticity can lead to well-being and happiness.

Chapter 4: The External Influences on Happiness

- **Social Connections:** Meaningful relationships provide belonging, resilience, and emotional support, enhancing overall well-being.

- **Environment:** Creating a positive physical, social, and emotional environment fosters happiness and reduces stress.

- **Purpose and Passion:** Pursuing activities aligned with values, contributing to others, and personal growth lead to fulfillment.

- **Resilience:** A sense of purpose helps navigate challenges, promoting emotional strength and optimism.

- **Balance:** Combining social connections, a positive environment, meaningful pursuits, and resilience contributes to sustainable happiness.

Chapter 5: Amplifying Serotonin Naturally

- Serotonin is a neurotransmitter influencing mood, emotions, and well-being, often referred to as the **"happy chemical."**

- It regulates mood, stress response, sleep, social behavior, appetite, and emotional resilience.

- **Lifestyle strategies** to increase serotonin include regular exercise, exposure to natural light, balanced diet, mindfulness, and social connections, acts of kindness, sleep, and creative expression.

- Cognitive techniques, such as positive affirmations, gratitude practice, reframing negative thoughts, mindfulness meditation, and visualization, can boost serotonin levels by changing thought patterns.

- Balancing lifestyle practices and cognitive techniques can naturally support serotonin production and promote emotional well-being.

Chapter 6: Boosting Dopamine for Lasting Joy

- **Dopamine** is a neurotransmitter associated with reward, pleasure, motivation, and learning.

- It plays a role in the brain's reward system, reinforcing behaviors through pleasure responses.

- Dopamine drives goal-directed behaviors, influences motivation, and contributes to feelings of accomplishment.

- Excessive dopamine stimulation from addictive substances or behaviors can lead to negative consequences.

- Balancing dopamine release through healthy pursuits, setting achievable goals, and avoiding excessive stimuli is essential for well-being.

Chapter 7: Fostering Oxytocin for Connection and Well-being

- **Oxytocin**, the **"love hormone,"** plays a pivotal role in social bonding and happiness.

- It is released during positive social interactions, promoting trust and intimacy.

- Oxytocin enhances empathy, leading to better social perception and understanding.

- It reduces stress, contributes to positive mood, and strengthens emotional connections.

- **Oxytocin facilitates parent-child bonding and plays a key role in romantic relationships.**

Chapter 8: Tapping into Endorphins for Pain Relief and Euphoria

- **Endorphins** are natural opioids produced by the body in response to stress or pain.

- They act as pain relievers, providing a sense of euphoria and well-being.

- Endorphins are released during physical activities, laughter, social bonding, and certain foods.

- Engaging in regular exercise, practicing laughter, connecting with others, and enjoying pleasurable activities can boost endorphin levels.

- Balancing endorphin release through healthy outlets contributes to pain reduction, stress relief, and improved mood.

Chapter 9: Creating Sustainable Joy

- Cultivate gratitude, positive affirmations, and reframing negative thoughts.

- Pursue passions, set meaningful goals, and engage in acts of service for a sense of purpose.

- Prioritize quality time with loved ones and maintain open communication.

- Show empathy, support, and care to strengthen relationships.

- Set healthy boundaries for work-life balance.

DISCLAIMER

This book is intended for entertainment purposes only. Readers are advised that the author does not provide legal, financial, medical, or professional advice. The content in this book has been curated from diverse sources. Prior to attempting any techniques outlined, readers are encouraged to consult licensed professionals.

By engaging with this material, readers agree that the author is not liable for any direct or indirect losses resulting from the use of the information contained herein, including errors, omissions, or inaccuracies. Compliance with all pertinent laws and regulations, spanning international, federal, state, and local jurisdictions, is the sole responsibility of the reader. Neither the author nor the publisher assumes any responsibility or liability for the reader's use of these materials. Any unintended offense to individuals or organizations is regrettable and unintentional.

****

ABOUT THE AUTHOR

Meet the visionary mind behind **"The Happiness Amplifier,"** *Mr. Girendra Nath Singh* is a distinguished Electrical Engineer with an MBA. Mr. Singh brings over three decades of hands-on industrial experience, both in India and abroad, to the forefront of his remarkable literary journey.

With a genuine desire to make a lasting impact, Mr. Singh's unique blend of technical expertise and unwavering dedication is woven into every page of his book. His commitment to crafting insightful narratives that resonate with readers is evident in **"The Happiness Amplifier,"** where he seamlessly bridges the realms of **psychology, neuroscience, and real-life experiences.**

Other books Mr. Singh has written:

Unleash Your Inner Creative Genius

https://books2read.com/u/bQe1Yv

****

Your Free Gift

As a token of my thanks for taking time to read my book, I would like to offer you a free gift:

Click Here or scan the below QR Code & Receive your Free Book:

https://gnsingh.ck.page/79606d929c

Thank You and a Small Request

Dear Reader,

I want to extend my heartfelt gratitude to you for journeying through the pages of **"The Happiness Amplifier".** Your decision to explore this book warms my heart, and I sincerely hope it has enriched your understanding of happiness and its intricate tapestry.

May I kindly request a brief moment of your time?

Taking a moment to leave a review is a simple yet impactful act that can shape the future of this book and the lives it touches. Please consider sharing your reflections on the platform where you obtained your copy.

Your support is a beacon of encouragement, and I am genuinely excited to read your thoughts and experiences. Thank you for being a part of this voyage towards lasting joy.

With heartfelt appreciation,

**Girendra Nath Singh
Author**

****